"Those who take the oath to serve our communities proudly do so . . . *BEHIND AND BEYOND THE BADGE* allows the reader to get to know officers who have taken that oath, many at a young age with no thought of what life after the badge looks like. I highly recommend reading all volumes of Donna's *BEHIND AND BEYOND THE BADGE* books."

ERNEST STEVENS
San Antonio Police Department (Ret.)
Emmy-winning HBO documentary main subject
Ernie and Joe: Crisis Cops
Best-selling Author

"Compelling real-life stories that humanize the badge. A must read during these challenging times."

SGT. DARREN BURCH (Ret.)
ID Channel's American Detectives
Host of FRN's *Badge Boys* Show
Author – *Twisted But True* book trilogy

Behind

and

Beyond

the Badge

Volume III

**MORE STORIES FROM THE VILLAGE OF
FIRST RESPONDERS WITH COPS,
FIREFIGHTERS, EMS, DISPATCHERS,
FORENSICS, AND VICTIM ADVOCATES**

DONNA BROWN

Storehouse Media Group, LLC
Jacksonville, FL

BEHIND AND BEYOND THE BADGE Volume III: More Stories from the Village of First Responders with Cops, Firefighters, EMS, Dispatchers, Forensics, and Victim Advocates

Donna Brown

Tallahassee, Florida 32317
www.BehindAndBeyondTheBadge.com
Donna@DonnaBrownAuthor.com

Ordering Information:

Quantity sales. Special discounts are available with the author at the email address above and type in subject line "Special Sales Department."

Publisher Information:

Storehouse Media Group, LLC
Jacksonville, Florida 32256
Hello@StorehouseMediaGroup.com

The views expressed in this work are solely those of the author and do not necessarily reflect the views of the publisher, and the publisher hereby disclaims any responsibility for them.

Cover design by Katie Campbell

Behind and Beyond the Badge Volume III / Donna Brown —1st ed.

ISBN-13: 978-1-63337-705-9 (hardcover)
ISBN-13: 978-1-63337-704-2 (paperback)
ISBN-13: 978-1-63337-706-6 (ebook)

Library of Congress Control Number: PENDING

Printed in the United States of America

Dedication

To All First Responders

"You cannot get through a single day
without having an impact on the
world around you.
What you do makes a difference.
You just have to decide what kind
of difference you want to make."
Jane Goodall

Contents

Introduction

In the first two books of this series, I was asked to include my story as it would lend credibility to them. Yes, I'm a retired police sergeant who served twenty-six years. I was a detective sergeant for fifteen of those years, ten of which I supervised my department's Homicide Unit. Sadly, I've seen the worst of what we as humans can do to ourselves and to one another.

But I've decided not to include my story in this volume. These books have never been about me but about the thousands of first responders who honorably serve and protect the communities they live in and love—those who do the job for all the right reasons. They are, without a doubt, the majority.

But it's also about humanizing them. Most people see only a badge. The person behind and beyond the badge is what, or more importantly, *who* they need to know. I truly had no idea how Volume I would be received, but the responses I received were overwhelmingly positive, and it opened so many doors for me to share this message on a larger scale.

Volume I gave me an unexpected platform of speaking engagements. I've spoken on college campuses to criminal justice students and professors, civic groups, women's professional groups, at bookstores, and most recently, to a group of readers via Zoom. No venue has been too small or too large.

These speaking engagements made it very clear to me that people had no realistic idea of what law enforcement officers do or what any first responder does for that matter. So I decided to write Volume II.

Once again, the responses were positive. So many people have reached out to me, some I would never have expected. A high school student who came to a book signing with his already purchased book in hand told me that he had read Volume I and asked if I would sign it. What an honor! This young man said that he was a police explorer with his local agency, had done some ride-a-longs, and wanted to be a law enforcement officer. My book was one that he felt gave him a true glimpse into what he might expect during his career.

A deputy reached out and said that it was nice to read about people who actually had done the job or were currently doing the job. Their thoughts validated his own; he was not alone.

A police officer told me that he and his wife had always felt that they had a great communicative relationship until they read Volume II together. She asked him if he had some of the same thoughts as those in the book's stories, if he felt the same way that they did, and if the job had that same effect on him. He told me that it opened up a new path for their relationship in such a positive way because he was now able to talk with her about things he had previously withheld from her.

A college professor told me that he had read the books, and they were like nothing he had read in the law enforcement field. He was encouraging his students to read them, especially if they wanted a career as a law enforcement officer.

A citizen with no ties to the first responder world, someone not particularly fond of police officers, told me that she came across Volume II and decided to read it. It gave her an entirely

2

new perspective on law enforcement officers and what they deal with over the course of their careers and opened her eyes to the toll it takes on them mentally, physically, and on their families. Additionally, she had never considered the other first responders that had been included in the book.

I could go on. But with each new contact, I realized just how passionate I had become about humanizing the badge and highlighting mental health issues, not just for those working as first responders, but also for the general public. The pandemic changed how we all went about our business, and I was no different. Podcast invitations came my way, and I've reached new groups of people and met some amazing folks along this journey, those just as passionate as I am and many even more so.

When the 2021 end-of-the-year statistics came out for line-of-duty deaths for law enforcement officers, it really wasn't a surprise for me. Sadly, the number-one cause of death was COVID-19. The second-highest cause of death was gunfire (https://www.odmp.org/search/year/2021).

What isn't counted as an official line-of-duty death is suicide. If it was, it would be, by far, the second-highest cause of death for 2021. It's a number that's been growing, not just for law enforcement officers but also for all first responders. We have to do better.

I have often heard from first responders that they don't talk about the job because people don't understand. And at times, this includes those closest to them. My response is that if we don't talk about these things, then they can't understand. And without understanding, little will change.

That's one of the things I love about the people in all three volumes of the *Behind and Beyond the Badge* book series. Each one of them willingly opened their hearts and let you in. For that, I will always be eternally grateful.

3

With each story I've written, I also have an immense sense of pride. These are my fellow brothers and sisters. But more importantly, I understand what each has given of themselves. Many continue to give even though they have moved on to phase two of their lives. I understand the physical and mental toll these jobs take.

The books are a mixture of active-duty personnel and those that have retired. Sometimes first responders struggle with retirement, and my hope is that many of these stories help those individuals realize that there is life after law enforcement or any first responder career.

I believe my books are different and have something to offer everyone. I hope you enjoy reading them as much as I enjoyed writing them.

To each of you, take good care!

ONE

Detective Dan Brite

Peer Support and Wellness Coordinator
Douglas County Sheriff's Office (Colorado): 8 Years
Lone Tree Police Department: 9 Years
Fort Lupton Police Department: 4 Years
Active Duty: 21 Years of Service

A longtime friend and former co-worker reached out and wanted me to meet his agency's new Behavioral, Wellness, and Occupational Health Coordinator, Nicole Troelstrup. The introduction was made, and she and I set a coffee date to meet and chat.

Nicole, who is also a licensed mental health counselor, told me that a deputy at her agency had provided her with my books. She had read them and wanted to meet me. We talked about her new position and the books. That led us to mental health for law enforcement officers and all first responders and humanizing the badge. Two topics that I'm passionate about.

She had made contact with a law enforcement officer in Colorado who is his department's wellness coordinator and was a source of information for her. Nicole thought he would be a great story for the third volume of *Behind and Beyond the Badge (BBB)* and provided me with his contact information.

Of course, I did an internet search on Dan Brite and discovered his amazing story. I sent Dan an email, introduced myself, told him about the books, and that I'd like the opportunity to tell his story. We did a FaceTime call and talked at length. Dan agreed to participate.

Dan served with the United States Marine Corps from 1994–1998 with an honorable discharge. In 1999, he graduated from the Aims Police Academy in Greeley, Colorado.

The Fort Lupton Police Department hired him in 2001 and so began his law enforcement career. Four years later, in 2005, he left to join the Lone Tree Police Department, a brand-new agency in Douglas County, where he served for the next ten years. Afterwards, in 2014, the Douglas County Sheriff's Office (DCSO) hired Dan, and he remains there today.

The year 2001 wasn't only about starting Dan's new career; it was also when he met his future wife Christy. Christy is now a sergeant at DCSO, which has since grown to 375 officers and approximately 375 civilian employees and volunteers.

Dan has had a variety of assignments and roles, which include patrol officer, school resource officer, field training officer, detective, and a long-standing member of SWAT. Along the way, he was promoted to the ranks of corporal and sergeant.

In 2012, Dan obtained a bachelor of science degree in organizational leadership from Colorado State University (CSU) and is working toward his master's degree in first responder and military psychology, also at CSU. He's projected to graduate in 2023 with a goal of becoming a licensed mental health therapist. I'll go into this in greater detail later in this chapter because it's an important part of Dan's story.

Everyone has a different reason for choosing the law enforcement profession. When I ask what they are, I always find their answers interesting. During our interview, Dan said, "Let's be honest. I joined this profession because the excitement of chasing criminals and the satisfaction of arresting those who preyed on the community energized me. I was contributing to something that was bigger than myself, and that fed my happiness and fulfillment."

With Dan's experience in a variety of positions, I asked him which one was his favorite. "It's a tie between SWAT and plainclothes detective," he responded. "Both positions were not only notorious for adrenaline dumps, but the camaraderie in those types of assignments is similar to that in the military. The brotherhood in both assignments was very strong and tight-knit, which I loved!"

I often delve into other questions at this point, but Dan's story is different. He had a life-altering incident and injury that makes his answers to some of those questions a bit atypical from others. Most certainly, they offer a different perspective.

The following is Dan's life altering event, in his own words:

"9/2/2016 at 2:29PM – I was working as a plainclothes detective and was on the DCSO regional SWAT Team. I was called from my home to respond to an address in Parker, Colorado. Information that was provided said the subject was intoxicated, addicted to pain medication, and was loading up his AK-47 assault rifle and other weapons. He told his wife that he was ready and willing to have a shootout with the police.

"The location of the incident posed significant problems. His address was a few hundred yards away from a hospital, middle school, elementary school, and a retirement home. Multiple units responded and set up a perimeter to prevent the subject from getting to any of these buildings. To make matters worse, both schools were about to release kids due to the school day ending. There were several parents lined up along the roadway waiting to pick up their children.

"Some patrol units got into an elevated advantage over the subject's property. With binoculars, they could see him loading his RV [recreational vehicle] with several weapons and ammunition cans.

"I arrived on scene and began donning my load-bearing SWAT vest, helmet, and M4 rifle. The vest only had rifle-rated plates in the front and back.

"The subject got into his RV and left his residence heading toward the middle school. There was a heavy police presence at a roadblock, protecting the school. That is where I was located when the subject saw the roadblock and began to make a U-turn, heading back toward his house.

"At that time, we did not know if he had other weapons at the house or if there were any potential hostages. We were tasked with isolating him away from the house to prevent him from gaining access. The Hostage Negotiations Team was enroute in hopes of talking him down.

"As he drove back to his residence, I was directly behind him with other plainclothes units behind me. We followed him into his driveway, and I immediately positioned my vehicle between his RV and the house with the goal of keeping him out of the house. Other units positioned themselves behind the RV and to the right and rear of the RV. Meanwhile, my wife, who is a sergeant with the same agency and a hostage negotiator, was enroute with the team.

"As soon as I put my vehicle in park, the subject began firing at me with his AK-47 while he remained in the RV. Due to my position, only he and I could see each other. I immediately began returning fire as I knelt down behind the left front tire of my vehicle. The subject climbed into the overhead compartment of the RV and got into the prone position as he continued to shoot at me.

"09/02/2016 3:11PM – 'Man down, man down. It's one of ours' was aired over the radio. I was hit with an AK-47 round on the left side of my chest, about four inches below my armpit, the one area that is not covered with bullet-resistant material. The round destroyed my spleen, half of my left lung, my diaphragm and came to rest in my stomach. I continued to return fire until I went unconscious. Officers were trying to determine who was shot, and someone quickly said, 'DB,' which was my nickname. Unfortunately, my wife was about fifteen minutes away from the incident and heard that over the radio. That is how she found out I was shot.

"Our SWAT team had medics within the team, and I am forever grateful that this SWAT medic, who worked for South Metro Fire Rescue, sprinted up the driveway as the subject began to leave in his RV. He quickly assessed me, and they threw me in the back of my vehicle to evacuate me to an awaiting ambulance.

"Meanwhile, the RV began driving through a field toward the hospital with several units following. I was driven to the roadblock where I was quickly transferred to the ambulance, and they took me to the hospital, which was only a few hundred yards away. Around the same time, the subject high-centered his RV on some landscape near the traffic light that led to the emergency room entrance. Two citizens, believing that the driver of the RV had a medical emergency, pulled over and went up to the driver's side of the RV.

"The subject exited the RV, turned around toward the citizen and said, 'Get the fuck out of here' as he began shooting at the hospital. Soon thereafter, two Parker police officers arrived on scene and eliminated the subject with a single shot. The subject was deceased, and the severity of the incident began to set in with a lot of the first responders on scene.

"I entered the emergency room doors with no pulse, and the doctors immediately performed an emergency thoracotomy. My doctor had previously worked in a hospital in Queens, New York, where they worked on gunshot and stab wounds on a daily basis. He was familiar with an emergency thoracotomy and had the skill set to save my life. They immediately opened up my chest and gained access to my heart. With his hands, he began to manually massage my heart. After a few seconds, they got it to beat again.

"They prepared to transport me to the operating room when I died a second time. They tried to put paddles on my heart and shock it back to life but were unsuccessful. The doctor went back to manually massaging my heart and got it to beat again. He gave me less than a 1 percent chance of surviving that night.

"I am going to pause here to explain the four things that occurred that led me to become a full believer in our Lord. Prior to this incident, I had so many questions about religion, and I wasn't convinced of a higher power. After my experience, I have no doubt for these reasons:

"Number one—An AK-47 round travels at roughly twenty-five-hundred feet per second. It is logical to believe that a round traveling that fast would continue straight through soft body tissue until it hits something hard. The round had an unob-structed path to the left side of my body and struck all soft body tissue. Not a single bone was hit, yet as soon as the round hit my spleen, it turned downward missing my heart altogether.

"Number two—Until I went unconscious, the subject was still firing at me. There were striations in the ground around me from the subject's rounds. It was as if Saint Michael was standing over me ensuring I wouldn't get hit a second time. Had I been hit with another bullet, I would not be here.

"Number three—When the suspect crashed in front of the hospital, he began shooting indiscriminately at the hospital. One of the rounds travelled through an office window, a computer screen, and two more walls before it stopped. That office was the office of the on-call surgeon, the only one who knew how to perform an emergency thoracotomy. Had he been struck, I would not be here.

"Number four—Having less than a 1 percent chance of sur-viving and overcoming those odds is astonishing to me. I fully believe the Lord intervened.

"I was in a medically induced coma for ten days. On 9/11/2016, soon after hundreds of community members held a prayer vigil outside my hospital window, I opened my eyes. I was under too much medication to really comprehend what had happened. In the coming days, I would learn that I was facing the biggest challenge of my life. In order to preserve my heart and brain, the doctors had to clamp the lower aorta of my heart to keep the blood flowing to the vital organs. As a result, the legs were starved of oxygen and blood both times they performed an emergency thoracotomy. This is why I am now permanently paralyzed from the belly button down. I was devastated to say the least.

"I immediately had ruminating thoughts of all the things I could no longer do. No more daddy-daughter dances, no more playing basketball with my daughters, no more holding my wife's hand as we go for walks, no more being a cop. All of my identity was being stripped away from me, and I was confused, angry, and lost. We were a two-income family; we had plans for an upcoming vacation; we had goals for retirement. We were your typical family.

"I went to Craig Hospital, which is a rehabilitation facility in Englewood, Colorado. A few days after I was admitted was the first time the realization of being paralyzed set in. They brought in a wheelchair and said that I needed to get into it so that I could go to PT [physical therapy]. I stared at the wheelchair. This was the first time I was presented with one, and I was now beginning to comprehend what life was going to be like. I refused to get into the wheelchair.

"The following day, they brought the wheelchair back. My wife convinced me to get into it. I pushed the wheelchair out of the room and about two doors down before I had to stop. Why am I so out of breath? Why is this so difficult? I had been a healthy two-hundred-twenty pounds before my injury. Now, I weighed one-hundred-sixty pounds with a large gaping hole on my left side that was still exposed. Muscle atrophy had set in, and I lost almost all my muscle. I realized what a long and hard road this was going to be.

"It was around this time that my mental health began to spiral downward. I waited at night for everyone to leave my room, and I would cry into a pillow. I tried my best to hide my emotions from others. I was afraid they would think I was weak. I was embarrassed to have such strong emotions because I have held it together for so many years. I barely spoke to anyone because my mind kept replaying the trauma over and over, and I didn't have the capacity to hold a conversation.

"Craig Hospital recommended that I stay with them for nine months, which meant I was going to spend Christmas in the hospital. I told the doctors that I wanted to be home before Christmas. They said I had to prove that I could take care of myself—that meant pushing the wheelchair, transferring to the toilet, taking a shower, and getting dressed. The everyday things. At Craig Hospital, your schedule is like a full-time job with doctor visits, tests, rehab, and physical therapy. On some nights and weekends, I would use the gym at the hospital to build up my strength. It was what I needed to accomplish most of the wheelchair tasks. In two and half months, I succeeded and went home on December 22nd.

"I was finally at home with my family. I thought this was going to help me overcome the mental health struggles. After the holidays, everyone went back to work and school, and I was left home alone. The negative thoughts kicked in again. I was angry, frustrated, overwhelmed with my new situation, sad for all the loss, and my mind would not stop thinking about it. At dinnertime, my family would talk to me, and I would stare straight through them and not respond. I couldn't pause the constant replay.

"Then I came up with the brilliant plan of coming back to work. A little over four months after dying twice and being paralyzed, on January 20, I was back at work part-time. This was the answer! I would be back with my team, back in the camaraderie, and back in a familiar environment as I was living my life in a very unfamiliar one. Things were going well.

"Then my plainclothes unit would often run out the door to handle some type of call. I was left behind for obvious reasons. Our offices were eerily quiet, and guess what showed up? Yep, the ruminating thoughts. Except this time, my mind decided to also focus on the fact that I would never be able to be with my team out in the field. I was going to lose my identity as a cop. Who can be a cop in a wheelchair?

"Things got worse mentally. My physical pain wasn't even an issue. I refused pain medication early on in rehab thanks to a Denver officer who had been shot five times. He shared his story with me about his injuries and pain medication. I immediately quit taking pain medication and learned how to deal with it. The nerve pain to this day is still very active, but it's not going to win!

"The worst thing was the mental anguish that was ripping me apart. I soon had suicidal ideation. I never developed a plan or decided how I was going to die; I just had thoughts of what if I died. It would be easier on my family as they wouldn't have to take care of me anymore.

"I was at my lowest point in life, feeling like I was hanging on by just a few threads. My wife couldn't take the yelling and arguments anymore. She too was suffering from caregiver fatigue, and she didn't know how to respond. She begged me to go to therapy.

"I was hesitant on our first visit. I didn't know the therapist, trust her, or feel comfortable sharing anything. I was just going to please her and share brief information so we could get out of there.

"Then I went a second time. Then a third. Eventually, I was going every week for almost two years. It was invigorating. A huge weight was lifted off my shoulders when I decided to stop avoiding my fears and thoughts and face them head on like I had with so many suspects I encountered in my career. I learned to challenge my thoughts and replace them with more accurate and positive ones, even if they were only slightly better. This allowed my brain to have the capacity to begin to enjoy the small things in life. Before, I was so engulfed with negative thoughts that I could never focus on even the smallest of wonderful things in my life.

"I remember the breakthrough. I was driving home from one of my mental health sessions. It was summertime, and the sun was setting over the Rocky Mountains. I looked at the sunset sinking behind the mountains and bouncing off the clouds, creating a surreal landscape that I was in awe of. I recognized that moment, I soaked it up like a sponge. I was able to enjoy that very moment, and what a relief it was to my mental state. That is when I made the decision to be 100 percent involved in improving my mental health and my relationships with my wife and kids.

"Five years later, and I still see a therapist on a regular basis. Yes, it was hard. Yes, I cried multiple times during sessions. Yes, I was afraid to face some of my thoughts. Yes, I was exhausted after many sessions. But I carried on because I learned to trust my therapist. She was very delicate in her approaches, and she was by my side the entire time. I didn't do it alone. If we hit barriers, we paused, addressed each barrier, and moved on. Sometimes we took steps back before we could move forward. Sometimes we moved at a snail's pace, and other times, we conquered things quickly.

"I can't express how important our mental health is and taking advantage of the healthy resources that are available. The stigma [against seeking mental health care] doesn't exist anymore; we just believe it does. I am proof of it. I am still a cop in a wheelchair and very vulnerable in sharing my experiences after the shooting. I have helped so many other first responders through the darkest of their days, and they overcame their struggles. There is plenty of proof that the stigma doesn't exist. We have to stop letting it dictate our lives, control our relationships, and destroy our careers. Let's conquer this imaginary stigma and live the life we deserve."

Dan sent me the above thoughts, and honestly, I had to read them several times. And when writing his story, I wasn't quite sure where to go from there. His life had dramatically changed. But having spoken with him, I knew that his thoughts about other topics would be equally compelling, especially those concerning his passion for mental health for first responders.

As Dan had said, his life changed drastically, and that included what he did to wind down and rejuvenate when off-duty. Pre-injury, his go-to destress activity was running. It allowed him to keep his emotions at a low simmer and not boil over. The runner's high afterward was very rewarding for him. He told me that post-injury, he really struggled because he could no longer run, and his only coping skill was not an option. It was an important life lesson for him, to have more than one coping skill in your pocket.

Now, Dan has new skills. "I enjoy fly-fishing, hunting, being outdoors in the sun, and taking family trips. I also practice mindfulness by focusing on my environment and being grateful for having the ability to still experience things that I enjoy. All of these new coping skills, along with therapy, have helped me overcome my deepest mental health struggles, including suicidal ideation."

Dan talks about driving and his ability to enjoy outdoor activities. Being paralyzed from his navel down, I had to ask why and how.

Dan told me this, "Once I found out I was permanently paralyzed, one of the recurring thoughts was having someone take care of me full time, and that negatively impacted my mental health. I was very independent before, and I wanted to stay independent, but I didn't think that could be possible anymore. I couldn't stop thinking about how much of a burden I was going to be on others.

"I can't say enough things about Craig Hospital. They do an excellent job of preparing you for life in a wheelchair. While I was in its inpatient rehab, they had a driving program where they taught me how to drive a car with hand controls, get in and out of vehicles, everything. It meant I got to keep a big portion of my independence. I was elated to learn that I could still drive, and it helped with alleviating the belief that I was going to be a burden on everyone. Worker's compensation covered the cost of outfitting my truck so I can drive."

Driving is one thing, and I have seen vehicles specially equipped like Dan's, but fly-fishing? Dan sent me some photographs and this explanation.

"The chair in the photos is an Action Trackchair that I got in 2017 through the Adsit Foundation [Adsitstrong.org] and the MC-1 Foundation. Both foundations found out that I really enjoyed the outdoors, so they made it happen."

(John Adsit was a Denver police officer who was struck by a car and spent several months in a hospital enduring multiple surgeries. He had to retire and created the Adsit Foundation. MC-1 was formed out of the line-of-duty death of Sergeant Baldwin with the Jefferson County Sheriff's Office.)

Dan continued. "The Trackchair allows me to still do the things that I love. I've parked it in a river for fly-fishing and taken it over rough terrain to hunt or to go on hikes. I even took it on a 5K run in downtown Denver one year while my wife and daughter ran. It is an amazing tool that provides me the freedom to get off the beaten path.

"With a wheelchair, I have to stay on concrete. The Trackchair allows me to go almost anywhere. Another organization is currently building a wheelchair accessible camper for me. We intend on loading the Trackchair into the back of the camper and getting back to enjoying the outdoors and what nature has to provide. Nature was another one of my coping strategies before my injury, and I am so happy that it will continue to be a part of me."

Dan has learned new coping skills post-injury, so I asked him what he personally did before his injury to keep his professional demeanor when on the scene of a particularly difficult incident.

He responded, "For many decades, this profession has taught an informal and often unnoticed lesson to new officers—how to suppress emotions to get the job done. New officers watch the veterans handle traumatic calls and remain cool. Through observations and conversations with veteran officers, we learn to emulate them, and quickly, we begin to emotionally blunt ourselves from the trauma.

"This is a very important survival technique and a skill we should continue to learn. However, what we need to add is when it's okay to emote, to share those feelings with family, friends, co-workers, and use resources to overcome the struggle. I was extremely good at emotionally detaching myself from some very traumatic calls. This allowed me to perform the tasks at hand and accomplish the job. But I never mentally dealt with the traumatic calls afterward and continued to stuff them down thinking that I would be good if I continued to avoid them. My shooting led to all of those emotions surfacing at the worst possible time."

I asked Dan what was the nicest compliment that he had received from someone he had helped. His answer surprised me. "I have been blessed with many compliments throughout my career. Perhaps the most impactful was after my shooting when I was in a wheelchair and wondering if what just happened was worth it. Then some parents in the community, who were complete strangers, stopped me in the grocery store and said, 'Thank you for saving my children' because they were in the nearby school when the shooting occurred. Their children could hear several gunshots when they were locked down and hiding in their classrooms. Their gratitude had a huge impact on my outlook on life and a unique way of energizing me and encouraging me to not give up . . . not to mention their gratitude caused my eyes to well up."

I always ask the first responders in my books what their career-defining moment was. Everyone has one, and some more than one, including me. My assumption was that Dan's would obviously be the shooting incident. I was wrong.

"I can identify the exact moment I decided to fight the stigma [of seeking mental health care] in this profession and to promote the importance of mental health.

"In 1996, I served with a United States Marine Corp (USMC) buddy until 1998. He eventually became a law enforcement officer in California, and I became one in Colorado. We talked on occasion and harassed each other on social media. After my shooting, he visited me at Craig Hospital during rehab. Not once but twice. He flew to Colorado, stayed at our residence, and spent almost every single moment at Craig. In fact, during my rehab, he was the only able-bodied friend who sat in a wheelchair because he wanted to know what it was like.

"We played lacrosse together, both of us in a wheelchair. That meant a lot to me, and I still cherish the picture of us together holding lacrosse sticks in wheelchairs. My buddy was unique. He had a very loud and deep voice, and you could hear him from far away. He was never afraid to voice his opinion, regardless of rank, and he wore his heart on his sleeve. He had one of the biggest hearts I have ever seen in a human. He only cared about you in the moment, and there was no use in asking how he was doing because, with his loud voice, he would flip it back to your well-being.

"During his last visit at Craig, we talked about our futures. He was planning to retire in the next few years and travel the country. He talked a lot about his beautiful family.

"In 2017, just eight months after my shooting, my buddy and I went to Police Week in Washington D.C. I was there supporting my agency for the line-of-duty shooting death of Deputy Zackari Parrish III that occurred on December 31, 2017. It was my friend's first-time visiting Police Week, and he was in awe of the brotherhood, camaraderie, and all the events that took place. We spent every day together, laughing, reminiscing about our military days, drinking beer, and paying respects to the fallen at the candlelight vigil. I have a photo of both of us at the vigil in our Class A uniforms. He looked sharp, and you could tell he took pride in the uniform. He even had his shoes polished to Marine Corps standards. You bet as a former Marine, I had to check him up and down to make sure he wasn't unsatisfactory! That was never the case with my buddy.

"On one of our last nights in D.C., we got to see a baseball game, one of his favorite sports. It was the Washington Nationals against the Atlanta Braves. He proudly wore his San Francisco Giants jersey, and we soaked up the ambiance. I can still hear his very deep laugh that was contagious. I also have a photo of him and me at that game enjoying ourselves. Little did I know, that would be the last time I would see him.

"A couple of days later, I received a phone call at about 3:00 A.M. I am a hard sleeper, so it took me a minute to wake up. The call went to voicemail. I checked the number, as I usually don't pay attention to unrecognizable phone numbers. But this was odd due to the time of the night.

"I checked my voicemail and learned that my buddy had died by suicide. I repeatedly replayed all my memories from Po-

21

lice Week with my buddy and tried to recognize any signs that he was struggling, but I couldn't identify one single behavior, emotion, or nonverbal cue that would indicate it. We had talked about my own mental health battles from the shooting—the anxiety, depression, PTSD, and suicidal ideation—but never once did he mention anything about his struggles. That was the frustrating part. He did such an excellent job at disguising his own internal battles, as just about every first responder does, that I never got a chance to connect with him on that level.

"That's when I decided my new passion was throat-punching this damn stigma in our profession and our society in general. For decades, mental health issues have been considered a weakness or means that a person is not trustworthy or can't perform their job. It is 100 percent impossible to live this life without any mental health struggles, especially for first responders. Every single person faces trauma in their life. Every single person faces loss in their life. Nobody is immune from mental health struggles.

"How is it then that our profession expects first responders to not have any mental health issues? The best thing we can do is offer them support and resources since the profession exposes them to so much more trauma than the average citizen.

"This is also when I learned that when we recover loudly, we keep others from dying quietly. This was a quote I saw by an unknown author, and it really resonated with me. I no longer keep my mental health issues quiet. I share them with everyone as a way to lead by example and show other first responders that it is normal to have emotions and that you overcome mental health struggles by addressing them appropriately."

With his new mindset, passion, and position within his agency, I asked him what was now the most rewarding or fulfilling part of his job. "Every day I am blessed to have an opportunity to not only still be in this profession while paralyzed, but to help my brothers and sisters in such meaningful and impactful ways," he said. "Although I can no longer help them on the street and stand by them when things get rough, I can help them from behind-the-scenes and be beside them in the aftermath. It is very rewarding to see a first responder overcome their mental health struggles, return to work, and flourish in their personal and professional lives."

Dan had told me that he is currently working on his master's degree, so I asked him to talk about his goals. He said, "In my current position, I respond to critical incidents that happen within the county and with any agency requests for our peer support or wellness team to assist with anything, including providing training, resources, critical incident support, or to help build wellness programs.

"My passion for mental health developed from my own struggles and the tragic loss of my buddy from the military. I decided it was time for me to be the change that I wanted to see in both professions. I wanted to be a part of the solution and not continue to feed the stigma.

"My wife and I are attending Colorado State University Global and are in the Military and First Responder Psychology Master's Program. This program was created by a very dear friend of ours, Dr. Sara Metz with Code 4 Counseling, and it is the first program of its kind in the nation. Her husband, Nick Metz, is also pretty cool!

"Sara is one of the best culturally competent first responder psychologists, and her passion for both professions is unparalleled. She also chooses to be a part of the solution.

"There is a severe lack of culturally competent therapists across the nation who can appropriately help first responders, veterans, and their families. The goal of this program is to help fill in the gaps of this shortage.

"Nick is a retired police chief, and he is the epitome of how leadership should approach the well-being of their first responders. He understands the mental health struggles of this profession, and he is not afraid to do what is right, even in the face of adversity. I admire that about him. "

With our discussions about mental health for first responders and everything that he had been through, I asked Dan what he thought was the most important quality to have to be a good law enforcement officer.

He replied, "This is a tough question because there isn't just one. Not only are being honest, transparent, and having sound morals all good qualities, but in order to survive this profession, one also needs emotional intelligence. This particular quality needs to be exercised more often than anything else because it is how you will manage the hundreds of traumatic events in your career effectively. It is how you will successfully navigate the collision between your personal and professional life to include marriage. It is how you create healthy coping strategies that get you through the difficult times on the job and help you enjoy the fruits of your labor well into retirement. We have to pay attention to our emotions and take care of them."

After Dan and I initially spoke, I sent him a copy of *Behind and Beyond the Badge: Volume II*, my most recent book, to read. Even though there are two volumes, they are stand-alone books that don't have to be read in order. I then asked him why he agreed to let me tell his story and be a part of *Volume III*.

"My goal of sharing my story is simple," he replied. "I share my experiences and the mental health struggle to show that we can overcome them, even in the worst of times. Sharing such experiences influences change within a culture. But I can't be the only one. As a brotherhood/sisterhood, we all need to share our struggles so others don't feel isolated and hopeless. This profession is awesome, but we have to take care of our mental health to ensure longevity that goes well into our retirement."

To help facilitate his passion for mental health for first responders and our military, Dan is a member of several board of directors and is active with other initiatives that include:

- Fraternal Order of Police Legislative Committee – focusing on the mental health of first responders in Colorado
- Board member for Colorado Fallen Hero Foundation – assists and supports family members of line-of-duty deaths
- Board member for It's a Calling Foundation – connecting first responders and veterans to mental health services, especially those who don't have the financial resources
- Commissioner for the Office of Suicide Prevention/Co-chair for the Governor's Challenge to Prevent Suicide Among Service Members, Veterans, and their Families – a program participated in by thirty-five states that is focused on suicide prevention in military populations
- Commission for First Responder Interactions with Persons with Disabilities – focuses on creating training curriculum at the academy and agency levels – based on HB 21-122
- Subject Matter Expert with the International Association of Chiefs of Police – helping agencies across the nation

build wellness programs (This is part of their CRI-TAC program.)

Dan said, "All of these provide me a platform to feed my passion in changing the mental health culture in first responders and for our veterans."

He has also received several awards for his heroic actions:

- 2012–Medal of Valor for a shooting incident on July 4, 2012: The award was earned when he was a member of DCSO SWAT, a regional team consisting of four law enforcement agencies, and working with the Lone Tree Police Department. Here is a link to the story: https://www.cbsnews.com/news/736-years-in-prison-for-man-who-shot-at-27-cops/.

Dan added, "Coincidentally, DCSO had been working for several months in getting the team a BearCat **(Ballistic Engineered Armored Response Counter Attack Truck).** The first day the BearCat was put into service, we had this shooting. The suspect was shooting at us with an AK-47, and the rounds were absorbed by the armored vehicle. Prior to the BearCat, all we had was a Yukon SUV, and nobody was safe from AK-47 rounds inside that vehicle."

All three of the below awards were for his shooting incident in 2016:

- 2016 – Purple Heart, Medal of Valor
- 2017 – Deputy of the Year
- 2018 – Congressional Badge of Bravery presented by United States Senator Cory Gardner.

Family is very important to Dan. Consequently, he shared, "My wife Christy is a sergeant at the same agency I work and is currently assigned to the Major Crimes Unit. At the time of my shooting, she was a sergeant in investigations and part of the Hostage Negotiations Unit. She responded to my shooting in that capacity, not knowing I was involved until she heard my name "DB" over the radio.

"Her experiences provide a unique perspective from a law enforcement spouse and someone experiencing caregiver fatigue. Simply put, she had to learn to put her oxygen mask on first before she could focus putting on mine. Christy is perhaps the strongest and most loyal wife I could have by my side. She is exactly what I needed to bounce back and find my passion. Yes, it does suck when your wife outranks you at work and at home. It's a small sacrifice though!

"I would be remiss if I didn't mention my two awesome daughters. We often don't consider the ripple effect of such an event involving a first responder. The focus is usually only on the person involved. To be perfectly clear, it affects so many people, including the family. It affected both of my daughters in their mental health, and they showed it in different ways and at different times. I love them both so much and am proud of how far they have come. I am very grateful to still be around to support them."

I always ask those who are in my BBB books if they have any final thoughts that they'd like to share. Dan responded by saying, "For the awesome brothers and sisters who are just entering this profession, this profession needs you! To ensure you stick around for the long haul, you have to take care of your mental health. You have to build a strong support system, and you have to be able to share your emotions and feelings with your trusted family and friends. Please don't keep this profession from them. The strength of your support system is arguably one of the best resiliency skills you can have. Seek mental health help early and often. Don't wait until you are faced with a crisis, have an alcohol addiction, or are on the verge of losing your job and family because of the stigma.

"For the awesome brothers and sisters who have been doing this for a minute, there is still time! I waited sixteen years into my career, faced numerous traumatic events, and suffered a life-threatening and life-changing injury before I decided to seek help. I wish I would have understood the benefits of mental health early on in my career.

"I still vividly remember my first suicide call, my first infant death, my first violent domestic violence attack with a bat, and my most gruesome fatal traffic accident. These memories stick with you for life, but the difference for me is that they don't control my life. I control my life as the memories aren't stuck on constant replay. That is directly due to seeking mental health help."

Thank you, Dan, for your service to your country and community.

Dan can be reached at: Lionsden0506@gmail.com

TWO

Officer Amiee Krzykowski

Berlin Police Department (Connecticut): 18 Years
Active Duty: 18 Years of Service

Law enforcement is a male-dominated profession and a department K-9 Unit's even more so. The number of female K-9 officers is increasing though, something that I'm happy to see. I'm a huge dog lover, and with the exception of my college years, I've never been without at least one dog in my home. The hard work, dedication, and the incredible trusting bond that officers have with their canines have always fascinated me. They hold a special place in my heart.

I wanted a K-9 officer in this book, so I started perusing mainstream and social media. A few K-9 teams sparked my interest, and I started following them. Aimee and her K-9 Casner was one of them. They work at the Berlin Police Department, an agency I knew nothing about. According to the 2020 census, the city of Berlin, Connecticut, has a population of 20,175 people and is approximately twenty-seven square miles. The police department has forty-two police officers.

Many of the first responders I've written stories about come from larger departments, but in reality, most departments are small. There are roughly 17,985 police agencies in the United States, and this number includes city police departments, county sheriff's offices, state police/highway patrol agencies, and federal law enforcement agencies. Approximately ninety percent of those agencies employ less that fifty sworn officers. There are about 900,000 law enforcement officers in the United States with twelve percent being female.

All these statistics combined played a role in my decision to reach out to Aimee. I told her that I was a retired police sergeant, the author of the *Behind and Beyond the Badge* series, I was currently writing Volume III, and that I wanted to tell her story. As with everyone who I approach about sharing their story, Aimee requested additional information, which I provided. She gave me an enthusiastic yes and quickly obtained permission from her agency.

Aimee told me that while she was in high school, she had envisioned a career path that didn't include law enforcement. Drafting and designing buildings were her plan. That changed one day when the Massachusetts State Police came to her school for a career day and brought all of their "toys." Those included helicopters, motorcycles, and their K-9s.

Aimee said, "When I saw the bond between a K-9 and the handler, I changed my career path, major, and college and decided to go into law enforcement. I have always loved dogs, and I grew up with a beagle. Despite the breed being notoriously stubborn, I spent time working with her and training her to do all kinds of tricks."

Aimee graduated from Western New England University (Springfield, Massachusetts) with a bachelor of science in criminal justice. Her entire goal of choosing the law enforcement profession was to become a K-9 handler.

After graduating from the Police Officer Standards and Training Counsel (police academy) with her recruit class #300, she was hired by the Berlin Police Department (BPD) in 2004. Even though BPD was an agency that didn't have a K-9 Unit at the time, she quickly discovered that she loved bringing order to chaos and helping people in their most difficult times.

She said, "It brought out a level of compassion and patience that I really didn't know I had."

During her first four years at BPD, she worked as a patrol officer, DARE (Drug Abuse Resistance Education) officer, and in the Detective Division. In the midst, in 2006, BPD established a K-9 Unit, and she applied. However, she was not accepted,

Aimee said, "Since law enforcement is a male-dominated profession, I continued to work very hard to earn my way on my merit. I wrote good reports, investigated cases thoroughly, and I believe I became a good cop."

But looking back to not getting the job with the K-9 Unit when she initially applied, she remarked, "In hindsight, it was obvious. I was too young and didn't have enough time working on patrol. I needed more time to mature and get a better handle on the job itself before having the added responsibility of being in charge of a four-legged animal that bites. I worked endless hours with the handler who was picked and helped him out with K-9 work, wearing the bite suit, laying tracks, and soaking up as much information as I possibly could.

Two years later, in 2008, a second K-9 position was created, and Aimee applied for it. She said, "I was competing against a few other officers who also wanted the position. After completing a grueling physical agility assessment, an oral board, and obtaining medical clearance, I got the job.

"I got to pick my dog from a vetted vendor. Utilizing a known vendor has its advantages. The dog comes with a guarantee that it's healthy, their hips are issue free, and it has the proper drive and temperament. If the dog doesn't pass the K-9 school, the vendor provides a new dog. But my first dog, Titan, met all those criteria, and we attended a sixteen-week K-9 training academy.

"The academy was filled with long days, wet feet, cold fingers, sweat-stained clothing, bathroom breaks in the woods, bruises, and dog bites, but I wouldn't trade it for anything. I remember after one particularly long, draining, and stressful day of training, Titan was sitting in a heel next to me. He was just as tired as I was, but he looked up at me with the most sincere expression and leaned into my leg for comfort. I melted. We had just become a team! Completing the K-9 academy was one of the most rewarding things I've done."

Titan was trained in patrol and narcotics. Aimee explained further, "A patrol K-9 is trained to track (find people) and locate evidence, which is anything that someone has touched like a gun, a knife, or an item someone may have thrown or discarded. K-9s are also trained to protect the handler and apprehend suspects. They're most often noted for taking down 'bad guys,' but 99 percent of the work we do with the K-9s is with their noses."

Aimee and Titan worked together for nine years. Titan was retired at ten years of age, and she was allowed to keep him.

She said, "Titan was a legend. A larger-than-life, loveable puppy turned big, bad police dog with an impressive stature and an old soul that everyone was drawn to. It didn't matter if you were an adult, a child, or a cat lover. Titan would win you over. He became a local celebrity and was on the front page of our local newspaper more times than I can remember. He had two retirement parties!"

When Titan was retired in 2017, Aimee wasn't guaranteed a new dog or a position in the K-9 Unit. Her chief was adamant that she wasn't going to get a second dog but that another officer would get an opportunity. But she applied for the vacant position anyway.

Aimee said, "I'm rarely dissuaded, so I put in my résumé and application. In my interview, I talked about the thousands of dollars of donations I had helped raise, community events I had participated in, suspect apprehensions with Titan, and criminal arrests made because of my dog. In the end, my chief had no choice but to agree that I was the best candidate!"

Aimee then began training Titan's replacement, K-9 Casner. "Casner has Titan's personality," she began, "with a much shorter attention span but a drive that is indescribable. Casner became his own celebrity quickly when a photo of us went viral. (Just do an internet search for 'police werewolf meme.') I appreciate Casner's differences from Titan as he has made me a better handler by challenging me in ways Titan didn't.

"I feel that being in the K-9 Unit has given me opportunities that I wouldn't have had if I had remained on regular patrol. I really use my ability to reach out to people who are drawn to the dog. We always joke and say that the canine officers are the most loved members of our department and that is 100 percent true. I do demonstrations with my dog throughout the schools, Cub Scouts, Girl Scouts, and citizen academies. I am always in the community eye. The different canine schools that I have been able to attend have really made me a more conscientious officer. They teach us different tactics and ways of doing things that makes our job safer."

There were two other reasons why I wanted to tell Aimee's story. One is that I believe she is an excellent role model for young girls and women who might be considering a career in law enforcement, especially as a K-9 officer. The other reason falls in line with my passion to humanize the badge and show the person behind the badge is just like everyone else and must deal with the same things that life's journey throws at them. Aimee is no exception.

Aimee was diagnosed with invasive ductal breast cancer at age thirty and a second time at age thirty-seven. She said, "Breast cancer is rampant in my family. I lost my grandmother, an aunt, and my mother to it, and my other aunt is a survivor.

"Even though I was only thirty years old, due to my family history, my primary care doctor suggested that I get a mammogram and ultrasound. I almost cancelled my appointment but begrudgingly went. The tests showed spots which they initially considered calcifications, but then I was sent for biopsies. They came back positive for cancer. I had a double mastectomy followed immediately by reconstructive surgery and hormone suppressing drugs for the next five years.

"I was only off the suppression drugs for about eighteen months when I found a lump. My recurrent cancer was removed, and I began chemotherapy followed by a course of radiation. Unfortunately, due to having a compromised immune system during chemo, I was out of work for about twelve weeks while I recovered.

"My father and I decided not to tell my mother about my diagnosis because she was so sick herself with breast cancer and under hospice care. That was rough, not being able to share my own diagnosis with my mother. She actually accused me of 'overplucking' my eyebrows. She just didn't know I had lost them during chemo. Then while I was still undergoing treatment, my mother lost her cancer battle.

"Chemotherapy was the worst for me because I'm a very active person, and I felt sick most days and couldn't get off my couch. Add the compromised immune system, and I had ear infections, bronchitis, pneumonia, and the added gift of a migraine at least once a week. I was so glad to get that junk out of my system. I made sure that on the days I felt well or at least semi-human, I would go to the gym, go for a walk, or take the dogs for a hike, anything to stay active and healthy. While undergoing radiation, I was finally starting to feel better and was able to start back to the gym more consistently though lightly.

"I was determined to build up my strength before I came back to work so that I wouldn't endanger myself or my coworkers. I had to be 100 percent before I would allow myself to come back. I'm stubborn, and a week after I finished radiation, I was back at work.

"I am very vocal about my journey because when I was first diagnosed, I felt that the cancer was a death sentence. I'm proud to show everyone that it isn't, and I will talk to anyone about it who needs some guidance, suggestions, or encouragement. Thousands of people are going through what I've been through. They're right there with me, and they need to know it's going to be okay. I've done numerous speaking engagements and photo shoots for cancer survivors to help boost their morale. I've brought a lot of awareness to the law enforcement community and general public about breast cancer, and I'm in charge of selling our departments pink uniform patches every fall for Breast Cancer Awareness Month. I advocate that mammograms save lives!"

While Aimee understands the importance of having a positive perspective, she also recognizes the added stressors that come with a law enforcement career. The horrific and often tragic things officers see can fill your emotional bucket quickly.

She said, "Everyone must have a healthy outlet. If not, that bucket will overflow. It's only been in recent years where mental health has become a focus in the law enforcement profession. There has always been an employer's employee assistance program, but nobody would use it. Our department started a peer-to-peer program for early intervention so that if you have something that's bothering you, there are resources available. We have counselors at our disposal that only work with first responders. For me, it would be difficult to talk about a particular incident or situation with a counselor who really has no understanding of what we do. I have definitely seen a positive shift that it's okay to talk with mental health professionals, and debriefings after critical incidents (where everyone involved can talk through the event) are now mandatory at my department.

"I stay active. Being outside is a must for me to decompress from work. I love to run, hike, and go to the gym and to the beach with my husband and friends. Every first responder needs to have that healthy outlet."

When Aimee mentioned her husband, I asked her to tell me more about her family. She said, "My husband and I got married this past year. He is a federal law enforcement officer, which makes it easier for us to understand the stressors of our jobs. We both understand the quick disconnect in the middle of a phone conversation when something is happening, and we understand the importance of saying 'I love you' when we leave for work or hang up the phone. We are fiercely proud and protective of each other, and we know that we will always support each other.

"My parents have been incredibly proud of what I do, even when I shield them from the crazy calls. My entire family, including my new in-laws, understand that my schedule is not Monday to Friday, and working holidays and weekends are sometimes mandatory. They adjust family dinner times so that I can attend them, and they understand when I can't be there. The understanding and support from my family is something I cherish.

"I love kids, but my type of cancer is fueled by hormones, and I've been on hormone suppressants for ten years now. Having children isn't an option for me, but my husband and I made the decision to keep our family to the two of us and of course, with the dogs!"

Aimee told me that she was excited to tell her story and hopes that people reading it will understand that law enforcement officers are human too. She added, "Officers are often portrayed as monsters in the media, but the vast majority are just good people doing a difficult job. We have families, take out the trash, grocery shop, cry at sappy movies, and get frustrated just like everyone else. We are doing our best in scary times.

"For my fellow brothers and sisters in blue, I wish you had the chance to work in my community. I feel respected and appreciated here in Berlin. Even when people may not agree with the outcome of an incident, it's the process they hate, not the officers. Change is happening in our profession, and not all change is bad, and sometimes it's necessary. Hang in there!"

Thank you, Aimee, Titan, and Casner for your service to your community!

Aimee and K9 Casner can be followed on Instagram and other social media platforms.
https://www.instagram.com/k9_casner/

Photo credit: Kim Carino Photography
https://instagram.com/kimcarinophotography?igshid=Ym-MyMTA2M2Y=

THREE

Police Officer First Class Carlyle Riche, Jr.

**Baltimore County Police Department (Maryland): 10 Years
Active Duty: 10 Years of Service**

When I wrote Volume I of the *Behind and Beyond the Badge* series, I was not a huge fan of social media. But I quickly realized from other authors and those trying to make a difference in the first responder world that having a presence on social media platforms was necessary. I created profiles for the book on a few of these sites and updated my LinkedIn profile.

I began posting about the book but became even more active once Volume II was published. I posted nothing political in nature and only positive things about the law enforcement profession and all first responders. That's still my personal rule.

My passion is to humanize the badge and that includes mental health issues concerning law enforcement and other first responders. I started following like-minded people and began making some amazing contacts.

That's how I connected with Carlyle on LinkedIn. I began noticing that we had a few common connections, and I started paying more attention to his comments. Carlyle then reached out to me, and we began chatting. His story interested me, and I did some research on the department where he works, Baltimore County Police Department (BCPD), and specifically, the unit that he is assigned to, the Behavior Assessment Crisis Management Unit (BACMU). I knew that I wanted Carlyle to be a part of *Behind and Beyond the Badge – Volume III*.

I told Carlyle a little more about the books and asked if he would be interested in letting me tell his story. He said yes but requested some additional details so that he could ask for permission from his chain of command. Permission granted!

Carlyle's decision to be a police officer was influenced by seeing the corrections uniform that his parents wore and his desire to help and protect others who couldn't protect themselves.

He said, "At a young age, I realized that individuals did have ill intentions and that I wanted to be that individual to confront them. I remember growing up and playing with friends in the neighborhood. When we would play cops and robbers, I always had to be the cop. It was a bit of an obsession for me. Each chance I got, I would run up to a police officer and express my interest.

"My entire family and those who knew me well knew that I would eventually become a police officer. It wasn't only about protecting others that led me to this career. I have always been interested in learning what makes people tick and why individuals behave in a particular way.

"I also felt it was important to 'be the change' I wanted to see in the law enforcement profession. For me, it was never about arrests or the persona of being a police officer; it was about finding real solutions for problems and building relationships between law enforcement and the community.

"I chose this career to protect others who cannot protect themselves. As I further it, I also feel that it's crucial to aid in changing the narrative for police officers. In my opinion, to do the vital work of building relationships with the community must be an unwritten rule for every law enforcement officer."

Carlyle was hired at BCPD as a police cadet in 2010. Cadets are individuals aged eighteen to twenty-one who are interested in becoming a police officer. They work in administrative positions until they reach twenty-one. They then undergo another short background check and must take and pass a polygraph examination. If they pass, they automatically attend the next police academy class.

Carlyle attended the Baltimore County Police Academy in 2011 and graduated fourth in the 136th recruit class. His career in law enforcement began as most do, working the streets as a patrol officer. He was assigned to the Woodlawn precinct and eventually became a field training officer.

In 2019, Carlyle applied for a position in the department's Behavior Assessment Crisis Management Unit (BACMU) and is currently assigned to the Mobile Crisis Team (MCT). He assists with other aspects of the overall unit but specifically with the Threat Management Team and with crisis intervention training.

To become a member of the BACMU, an officer must have completed their probationary period and then a forty-hour block of crisis intervention training and a Critical Incident Stress Management course. They must also pass a rigorous assessment process that includes knowledge, skills, abilities assessment, writing assessment, resume evaluation, and a situational interview assessment. It's a fairly competitive process, and an officer must have an interest in mental health and crisis response.

Carlyle explained, "The BACMU is comprised of many different facets, including the Mobile Crisis Team, Threat Management Team, Critical Incident Stress Team, Peer Support and Wellness Section, and the Crisis Intervention Training team. The BACMU is also a facet of the Baltimore County Crisis Response System (BCCRS).

"Our local Department of Health contracts with a local mental health agency that supplies the mental health clinicians and outpatient mental health services that make up BCCRS. In essence, the police officer structure is provided by the BACMU, and the contracted mental health agency provides the mental health structure. When we marry those two together, both components make up the BCCRS.

"The BCCRS provides the clinicians that make up MCT, the crisis hotline, the Urgent Care Center, and the In-Home Therapy team. With the twenty-four-hour crisis hotline, an individual can talk with a phone counselor. That counselor has access to many mental health resources, can help clients process difficulties/ trauma/emotions via the telephone, and send a MCT to speak with the client in person.

"The Urgent Care Center is not like a stand-alone medical facility. It is a resource housed in our office that allows citizens to obtain an assessment by a licensed clinician, possibly being escalated to our in-office psychiatrist for medication management. The service is free of charge to area residents, and the unit does not schedule anything past forty-eight hours. An Urgent Care Center appointment allows us to be an effective bridge to further mental health support.

"Suppose someone can't get an appointment with another community mental health provider due to waitlists or other barriers. In that case, someone can be assessed within forty-eight-hours by one of our clinicians to assist them in finding an area provider for more long-term support. If they cannot be linked to an area mental health provider, they can then work with our In-Home Therapy team, which is comprised of licensed clinicians who can work with an individual on a more ongoing basis. This service is still a temporary option until an individual can be linked to an area provider; however, it is another attempt to link clients with mental health support."

The Mobile Crisis Team was formed in 2001 as a pilot program on the east side of Baltimore County, Maryland, where one team would service a portion of Baltimore County. The goal was to provide a comprehensive response to community members with mental health challenges, increase linkage to mental health services in the community, increase a patrol officer's options in handling mental health-related calls for service, and limit the exposure of those with mental health challenges to the criminal justice system. The Mobile Crisis Team operates a co-responder model that pairs a specially trained police officer with a licensed mental health clinician.

Carlyle added, "My role within the unit is to respond to mental health-related calls for service with my clinician partner. I'm an integral part of the multidisciplinary team and am tasked with ensuring a safe environment for my mental health clinician partner. When we arrive at the scene, my partner and I begin to build rapport with our clients and attempt to learn their stories. This is a crucial part of our duties because it allows us to tailor our plan to the client and their needs at that moment."

The Baltimore County Mobile Crisis Team has had nothing but upward motion. Funding has been increased multiple times to allow for more teams. Present day, the Mobile Crisis Team has expanded to reach the entire county with, at times, four teams on the road responding to mental health-related calls in the community. In 2021, the Mobile Crisis Team handled 1,439 calls for service with an average response time of seventeen minutes across Baltimore County's 682-square-mile jurisdiction.

Carlyle said, "The team wears a more subdued uniform compared to our patrol counterparts. The goal is to lessen the mental health stigma that may come with a traditional police response. The team drives unmarked police vehicles.

"In our unit, on the police side, the team is comprised of about twelve officers and five supervisors. The local mental health agency side comprises approximately twenty full-time and part-time mental health clinicians who work in varying parts of the organization. We operate on a twenty-four-hour basis with as many as four teams on the road to respond to mental health-related calls for service, depending on the time of day. We work eight-hour shifts, and our schedule mimics the department's patrol division, including weekends and holidays. There is no need for an on-call designee because we always have an MCT on the road to respond to calls."

The law enforcement response to mental health-related situations has received an increasing amount of media attention, both positive and negative. What BCPD is doing as an agency and Carlyle's passionate role is one of the reasons I wanted to tell Carlyle's story. I asked him for additional details about the BACMU.

He responded, "One of the main functions is to divert individuals experiencing mental health challenges from the hospital emergency room. We have seen a revolving door of individuals with mental health challenges being sent to the hospital and released shortly afterward. We acknowledge our client's feelings about losing their autonomy and being forced to be assessed in a restricted hospital setting. We also acknowledge the importance of giving our clients the necessary tools and services to support them to keep them in the community and a familiar environment rather than being relegated to hospitals and psychiatric wards.

"This task is accomplished by conducting crisis assessments in the field and can often divert people from the hospital and create a safety plan with the client, provide psychoeducation, and give an overview of what available support may fit their specific needs. These assessments can be conducted in the client's environment— in their home, in alleyways, on the street, or under bridges. We meet them where they are, which is an excellent aspect of our unit.

"In 2021, we diverted 307 individuals from the hospital and kept them in their familiar environment. When we can create a safety plan with the client, we follow up with them the next day to ensure linkage to mental health support. Follow-up can continue for as long as the client requests.

"There are situations where our clients require a higher level of intervention, which entails us going to the nearest hospital to undergo a mental health assessment. This is where I believe the co-responder model (specially trained police officer and mental health clinician) shines. When the client necessitates an emergency petition (civil commitment for a mental health evaluation), the team already has an individual (the police officer) on the scene who can handle the custodial aspect of this interaction. The clinician can then step back and complete the civil commitment paperwork while the officer can engage with the client and navigate any ambivalence or questions posed by the client.

"In my opinion, co-responder teams have their place in the crisis response field. With these teams, the mental health clinician is not required to step back and dial 9-1-1 to get a police officer to respond to the scene. I acknowledge events across the country with the police response to individuals with mental health concerns. If a single clinician responds and needs to call 9-1-1 for an officer to respond, they may not know the officer's training in mental health topics or their ability to safely get that client the assistance they require. With our co-responder teams, the clinician knows that the officer they are partnered with is trained in mental health studies and de-escalation and has a shared interest in helping clients get the support they require.

"Our team sometimes interacts with individuals who don't have insight into their mental health challenges, individuals who may even be experiencing hallucinations or delusions. These aspects create barriers that must be traversed with the individual that necessitates an involuntary mental health evaluation in the hospital. That individual may vehemently express that they aren't willing to go to the hospital; however, that officer on scene has been there from the beginning of the call, has already taken steps to build rapport, has training in the perspective of someone experiencing mental health challenges, and can deploy de-escalation strategies to gain voluntary compliance.

"In 2021, out of 1,439 mental health-related calls for service, only two calls required the MCT officer to use force to get a subject to the hospital. The biggest tool that our unit uses is verbal tactics. It's crucial that we take the time to get to know the client before engaging in an assessment. Our calls often take one hour from start to finish and the bulk of that time is spent building rapport with that client. Frequently, individuals in crisis want to feel heard and get things off their chest, and we welcome that.

"Other duties of the team involve diverting psychiatric patients from possibly unnecessarily being sent through the criminal justice system. Most of our calls for service come from patrol officers in the field. If an officer is handling a criminal complaint and they suspect a mental health component is involved, the officer can request MCT to respond to conduct an assessment. There are times when someone's behavior can be the result of mental health challenges; therefore, on some calls, MCT can guide that individual toward mental health support rather than charging them criminally for the precipitating behavior. In 2021, MCT was able to divert forty-one individuals from being criminally charged in court.

"Each member of the MCT is trained in Critical Incident Stress Management and acts as a Critical Incident Support Team (CIST) member. CIST members can be deployed to process (talk, work through something) with individuals following critical incidents from natural disasters, death of loved ones, death notifications, traumatic events, or any other event that conjures a significant emotional response. In 2021, MCT handled approximately 178 CIST-related duties and conducted follow-ups with those clients to offer further mental health support."

It is clear that Carlyle is passionate about his job, so it was no surprise when he said, "By far, my favorite position has been on the Mobile Crisis Team, a position that I take seriously. A CIT officer is an officer trained to effectively respond to crisis events and is knowledgeable of the various avenues to guide an individual toward additional support.

"The topic of police response to mental health calls has been under intense scrutiny lately and for the right reasons. I agree with many of the sentiments and recommendations for change. I take pride in being a first responder who can viably and effectively respond to mental health or crisis-related calls for service. I believe it takes a particular person to be able to serve someone in that capacity and that unique quality is enhanced when you have experienced mental health challenges yourself. That individual can listen more intently, practice empathy, and walk with that individual through their experience, a great example of the support necessary in these intense situations.

"I'm particularly passionate about crisis response and adding to the narrative that some officers can effectively respond to mental health or crisis-related calls for service. I'm also enthusiastic about training and helping officers who may feel ill-equipped to respond to these calls for service. Currently, I assist with crisis intervention training for my department, and I co-teach de-escalation, a self-developed course for police officers. De-escalation is also a topic I feel strongly about.

"During this training, we walk officers through the process of de-escalation. Our goal is to have officers understand how de-escalation works, their role in de-escalating intense encounters, and how that benefits everyone involved.

"I was recently named Baltimore County's Crisis Intervention Officer for 2021, a highlight of my career thus far and an honor that I do not take lightly. I take pride in being a CIT officer. Some advocates believe that police officers do not belong on mental health or crisis calls and that civilian-only response teams should be used for these calls. I understand this sentiment; however, I believe that officers have their place on crisis teams. With training and awareness, an officer can be an equal partner in getting someone to the next level of support. I strive to advocate for this sect of police officers further."

Carlyle is in a unique position as mental health units are not the norm at the majority of law enforcement agencies although more are trending in that direction in some variation. The most difficult part of the job for Carlyle is navigating situations where individuals may not trust or are skeptical of law enforcement.

He said, "I see it as a personal mission to help those outside of the profession recognize that not all officers are the same. I respect that individuals are situated in their viewpoint or have had prior experiences (possibly negative) with law enforcement. I believe that's important for every police officer to note when interacting with the public. In those situations, I hope to give citizens a different perspective of police officers and leave them better than how I found them. However, I acknowledge that this cannot always be achieved during every interaction with the public. This is the most challenging part of the job for me, having to be okay with others having preconceived notions about me without knowing me or my intentions."

Law enforcement officers have direct contact with people every day in a wide variety of situations, more so than any other profession. One thing is constant and that is remaining professional no matter the scenario. I often ask people what they personally do to remain focused and professional in the most challenging situations.

Carlyle answered, "As with any police call for service, we are not always called when someone has a great day. The same goes for any crisis response field. Our clients are often experiencing the worst days of their lives, and we are regularly called to traumatic or chaotic scenes. It is vital for an officer to have a firm grasp on their own self-care, to have an intimate knowledge of their triggers, and recognize when they are reaching the point of burnout.

"Personally, these are aspects that keep me grounded during complex incidents. This is one of the significant aspects of working on our calls for service as a team. If one team member becomes triggered or has a tough time during a call, we can transition and support one another to get the job done.

"Debriefing after the call is also a necessary component. What went well? Are there things that affected you? What could have gone better? These questions help me process through difficult calls and prepare for future calls for service.

"Taking myself or my ego out of the equation is also helpful during complex incidents. I often have to realize that someone else's behavior is not a result of me. It could have something to do with my professional identity; however, I need to recognize that someone's reaction toward me is not a personal attack. This mindset helps me remain objective and rational and not ruled by my emotions."

Carlyle told me that compliments from citizens have had a profound impact on him. He takes pride in attempting to give others an alternate attitude about law enforcement officers as he aims to treat others like he does his own family and how he would like his family members to be treated.

He recognizes that many influences can affect a person's view of law enforcement, and he respects those different perspectives. His belief is that viewpoints drive who we are and what we do.

When he encounters someone who has expressed their distaste for law enforcement, he said, "I find it essential to flow with that interaction instead of fighting against it and becoming defensive. My father was also in law enforcement, and I remember him saying that it is not a personal attack when others express how they don't like or appreciate law enforcement. Their emotions are toward the position you occupy, the authority you have, and the shield you carry. It's not always about you. As a result, their feelings and emotions are based on their past socialization, and we are all entitled to our opinions. We can disagree but still respect one another.

"During interactions where someone has expressed negativity toward law enforcement, I feel that's a perfect opportunity to lean into that line of communication and help provide an alternative way of looking at us. That other individual is entitled to their outlook, and it is essential to note that I also feel that law enforcement officers are afforded that same courtesy. Sometimes, providing context for why we do what we do or other decisions made in the field is enough to fill in those gaps in that citizen's story.

"If we do not capitalize on those crucial moments, naturally, one's brain fills in that narrative with commentary based on their mindset. I enjoy interactions such as these. It's the perfect opportunity to help bridge that gap between law enforcement and the community. A message to other police officers: Let's provide that alternative narrative."

Carlyle understands that working in the law enforcement profession can make someone cynical, jaded, and callous at times. But he believes that being an effective officer means remaining compassionate and striving to develop their own sense of empathy.

He said, "I believe that as a police officer, it's essential to recognize the world's ills. However, I also believe it is equally important to acknowledge the good in others. As I reflect on this, I'm reminded of the words of Mahatma Gandhi, 'You must not lose faith in humanity. Humanity is like an ocean; if a few drops of the ocean are dirty, the ocean does not become dirty.' In this profession, I believe it is essential to recognize that there still is good in the world, despite the reminders of the evil that can occur and that we see every day."

Every law enforcement officer and first responder has had what I consider a career-defining moment. As I have stated in other stories, some people have to think about this when I ask what theirs might be. Some don't hesitate and can recall exactly what that moment was. Others have more than one. For Carlyle, he talks openly about two situations that had a profound impact on him.

He said, "I remember having just completed the field training program and was about twenty-two years old at the time. One night, I handled a domestic-related call for service where reportedly a husband and wife were arguing. It was a reasonably common call. Still, an officer should always practice good officer safety skills in responding to these situations.

"The call appeared simple, an argument between spouses. Both parties were calm upon my arrival. The situation appeared to handle itself as the husband elected to leave the home and stay at a friend's home to quell the argument for the night. Both parties were agreeable. I documented the incident as required, made follow-up notifications to our domestic violence coordinator, and then cleared the call.

"The following day, I was loading my police vehicle to begin my early morning day shift. A call went out over the police radio for shots fired at the address I was at the previous night. The call indicated that the husband came back to the location and shot his wife in front of the family and then fled the location. As police units were headed lights and sirens to the location, my head was swirling with thoughts and feelings about this call. Did I miss something? What could I have done differently? What would happen to me knowing I had just been to the house?

"When I arrived, the family on the scene immediately began shouting that the husband had fled in his vehicle and mentioned that I had just been to the home the previous night. After medical services arrived on the scene, I left the primary and backup officers there and began to canvas the area for the subject since I knew what he looked like. Similar thoughts were still swimming around in my head, and the adrenaline was pumping.

"One unit found the subject's vehicle driving down a busy street during early morning traffic. As other units began to tail the subject, we started formulating a plan to conduct a felony stop. Before the initiation of the stop, the subject became aware of our presence and began driving at a high rate of speed away from us, only to crash into a pole a short distance away.

"As units began to set up to approach the vehicle, we heard a gunshot from inside the vehicle. After ensuring that all officers on the scene were okay, we started calling out to the vehicle but received no answer. As we began our tactical approach, we immediately noticed the subject alone inside the vehicle, slumped over in the driver's seat and suffering from an apparent self-inflicted gunshot wound to the head.

"We secured the subject and requested emergency medical services. Seeing the male subject's lifeless body conjured many emotions for me, considering I had just seen him alive the night prior. The female half of that incident survived her attack after numerous facial surgeries. After more than eight hours in a trauma center, the male was declared deceased.

"This incident was challenging because I was a young officer, and I had responded to that house the previous night. It was such a graphic scene for a suburban kid from New Jersey who moved to Maryland for college and wanted to make a difference in the world. That day, I realized how evil people could be and the extreme dangers this job can hold. The images of this scene are etched into my memory to this day. After processing it in therapy, I realized that I couldn't have done anything differently the night I handled the initial domestic call. Without a crystal ball to predict the future, I would have made the same decisions considering the information I had at the time."

Carlyle then shared his second career-defining moment. "The other incident occurred while I was working an off-duty secondary job at a shopping mall. I was at the end of my shift and was preparing to leave when I heard a security officer yell over the security radio that someone had jumped from the fourth floor of the mall down to the first. Initially, I could not confirm what I had just heard, and then the security officer uttered the same comments again.

"I ran down to the bottom floor of the mall while directing additional police and medical units to the scene. When I got to the bottom floor, I saw a young male unresponsive with tremendous trauma to the head. The image is still burned into my mind. Crowds started forming around the railings on the floors above all yelling for me to do something.

"This young man suffered extreme trauma from the more than fifty-foot fall. He had limited eye movement and very shallow breaths. I was trying my best to assess what, if anything, I could do until the medical teams arrived. I carry an individual first aid kit (IFAK) but the amount of gauze and clotting agents I had was insufficient to lessen what this young man had endured.

"Before the first unit arrived, which seemed like an eternity but was only about three to four minutes, the young man stopped breathing and was completely unresponsive. Soon after that, he was pronounced dead on the scene.

"When units and medical personnel arrived, I learned that the young man was accompanied by his friends, who were trying to process what happened. At that point, I went into 'mobile crisis' mode, brought them all back to the security office, and began to provide initial emotional support as well as identify who I could contact on their behalf. I also reached out to the on-duty mobile crisis teams to assist.

"After an investigation into the events, it turned out that this young man had some significant mental health challenges and suicidal ideations involved that prompted this tragic event.

"I suppose that because of my interest in mental health and this individual's age, this incident hit hard for me. I cannot imagine what the individual was going through that prompted the desire to die by suicide. I cannot imagine the pain and belief that this was the only way to ease that pain. I cannot imagine what the individual's family and friends had to endure that day and during the grieving process afterward. I feel for the bystanders who witnessed this horrific scene, and I continue to pray for all those affected by this tragedy.

"I began to process this event after I was cleared from the scene. Was there a point when I walked by this young man during my shift and made contact with him? Could I have done anything? Was there a life-saving tactic that I could have deployed to prolong his life a little longer? I soon recognized that this was twenty-twenty hindsight, and there was nothing I could've done differently, but these questions still stuck.

"This event was a significant experience for many reasons but two in particular: First, it's okay to feel. Second, I realized the importance of support in the face of trauma or adversity.

"I've pondered how first responders typically respond to critical incidents such as this one. I directly witnessed what it felt like to turn outward during a high-stress situation. I immediately 'compartmentalized' what I was experiencing because of the incident and turned my attention to what needed to be done for others. This is the hallmark of being a first responder—service before self.

"For some reason, this event was different from any other critical incident I've been involved in. I immediately 'stuffed away' critical feelings and emotions that could help me process what had just happened as I had a job to do.

"This idea of 'compartmentalization' is necessary for first responders because it allows you to get the job done. However, as I reflect on this notion now, I wonder how effective this is in the long run. It was a long time before I brought this incident up in therapy. It was a long time before I 'decompartmentalized' this event in my head to allow myself to process what occurred. I now wonder how those who do not acknowledge their own mental health or those who fall into the old-school law enforcement mental health stigma of 'suck it up and move on' may have traversed this situation. I did not allow myself to process this moment soon enough and carried this event with me for a long time. As first responders, we must find healthy ways to process some of these horrors.

"Regarding support for others, I frequently think about this day and the sights seen. I believe I am in a better place having confronted those emotions in a supportive environment and for having received an abundance of support from my coworkers and supervisors. In my opinion, there is nothing more valuable. My captain came to the scene to check on me, even though it was his day off. I'll never forget that. I was fortunate that these coworkers and supervisors continued to check on me during the incident and many times afterward.

"Human beings are social creatures and require that connection at times. I believe this is especially important during times of stress, despair, and in the face of traumatic events. We are not meant to navigate these situations alone. It's okay to accept help from others.

"I remember when a client said to me, 'I can't bring myself to ask for help from you.' I replied, 'That's okay. You don't have to ask.' I recognize the pride that we may have, especially individuals in the first responder profession. We need to realize that we are not meant to handle all of life's challenges alone, and maybe, God has placed this specific event in front of us to test our ability to ask for help.

"I can't imagine getting through some of the critical incidents that I have been involved in without not only the support and assistance from my coworkers and supervisors, but also from friends and family. I remember processing one of these events with my father, and he mentioned, 'You've seen a lot in just a short career thus far. Trust and believe this will make you a better man and police officer.' That has always stuck with me. It's okay to walk through these challenging moments with others, we are not alone."

It is crucial for all first responders to make the time to do things to de-stress from the daily mental and physical rigors of the job. I asked Carlyle what he did to rejuvenate.

He said, "At the beginning of my career, I was excited to be a cop. When I had days off from work, I couldn't wait to get back to work. As soon as I received approval from the department, I started working secondary employment for security agencies that hired off-duty police officers. But the more time I spent on the job, I began to realize how important time away from the job was and that I needed and wanted other hobbies and experiences outside of law enforcement.

"As a child, I was a quiet, introspective kid, and I quickly found 'my thing' that allowed me to express myself ,and that was music. Since the second grade, I have played the piano and soon transitioned to drums. I played in various bands throughout middle school, high school, and college. Music is my way of expressing myself when words fail.

"Looking back, I owe it to music that I did not follow the wrong crowd or get into trouble because I always had music rehearsals or performances. I owe it to my mother for signing me up for my first piano lesson. Music remains a way that I de-stress outside of work. I don't play in any bands, but I regularly play my piano."

I asked Carlyle why he agreed to let me tell his story and what he hoped those who read this book would gain from it.

He said, "When you initially approached me about being in this volume, I was immediately excited and eager to participate. As I've consistently said, the topic of police crisis response is a tremendous passion of mine and something that needs to be talked about and improved upon. That's one thing that I hope law enforcement personnel and mental health practitioners gain from reading this. In my opinion, adversarial and strained relationships need to be eliminated and a path toward working together to serve a population that needs our support and assistance must be forged. I hope to continue to have a seat at this table and participate in these discussions, and I appreciate the light that is being shined on this topic.

"I highly support departmental peer support and wellness initiatives and those creating their own units or departments. As a profession, this is long overdue. I also hope that people will understand the importance of their own mental health and self-care. The old beliefs of 'suck it up' need to be eliminated. Yes, you have to do that to take care of the job at hand, but after that, your mental health matters. I believe in the common saying of 'It's okay to not be okay' because it is. It's okay to be broken and to work your way back to being whole. It's okay to cry, to hurt, and to feel. As first responders, we are human first. There is support out there, and I'm excited to see the profession beginning to pivot in that direction."

Carlyle also believes in giving back and trying to be a support system to others outside of law enforcement. For the past twelve years, he has been a volunteer youth counselor and a diversity, equity, and inclusion co-advisor for the American Legion Jersey Boys State (ALJBS) program in Lawrenceville, New Jersey. This program is geared toward high school juniors. It's a selective, week-long, college preparatory leadership seminar that can prepare its participants for careers in politics, the military, business, and law among many other professional paths. He is a lead youth counselor and senior staff member that manages the day-to-day instruction of a group of young men for that week along with other assistant counselors.

Carlyle told me why this is important to him. "I attended the ALJBS program when I was in high school and have been returning as a staff member ever since. I learned so much about networking and public speaking during my time there. I enjoy helping mold young men into the future leaders of America. I also volunteer for the Greater Chesapeake Chapter of the YMCA in Baltimore City, the Baltimore County Police Youth Leadership Academy, and the Big Brothers Big Sisters of America, which I am passionate about. I've been a mentor in this program for about three years. Words cannot describe the sense of pride in supporting my mentee. I don't personally have a little brother, so it's great to be in a position to impact my mentee positively.

"My mentee and I were matched well and have similar interests. He's an introvert just like me, and I've been able to share what was helpful for me at his age to help him pass through obstacles in his life. It's been wonderful seeing him grow and overcome many challenges in our short time together."

Carlyle has future goals that align with the mental health field. He said, "Being involved in my current unit has led to my desire to obtain further education in the mental health field and aspire to be a practicing mental health clinician. In 2017, I graduated from the University of Maryland with a bachelor of science degree in criminal justice. I hold a master's degree in criminal justice with a concentration in behavior management (St. Joseph's University, 2020), and I'm currently pursuing a secondary master's degree in clinical mental health counseling.

"I have a passion for mental health and consider myself a mental health advocate. I aspire to have a more profound impact in the mental health field and support others battling challenges that can seem unbearable. I'm a strong proponent of therapy, especially for first responders. I acknowledge that I am in therapy as well because I hope it helps normalize getting mental health support.

"As a first responder, I recognize that we are frequently exposed to traumatic events and that the profession has not always acknowledged the impact these events can have on one's mental wellbeing. I appreciate that mental health support is becoming a topic of discussion within the first responder community, and I am excited to aid in that endeavor.

"First responders are often indoctrinated into a culture that ignores the aftermath of some of the sights seen during a tour of duty. These invisible wounds are often ignored or dealt with in an unhealthy manner. I aim to be a mental health support for those within the profession.

"Trust is important as it relates to the first responder community, especially for someone seeking mental health care. I believe that my experience in the first responder community will help in my ability to serve others in the profession. I understand those invisible wounds, and I hope to have a private practice one day where I can support those in need of mental health services."

Carlyle is adamant that his parents truly made him the person and man that he is today. Both of his parents were correctional officers and met while working at the same facility. They instilled in him the importance of respect and discipline.

He said, "My mother and father are still alive, and I have a great relationship with them. They are the most supportive parents I could ever ask for. They have been my biggest cheerleaders, especially during the many times when I struggled to believe in and be excited for myself. I still strive to be the best I can be for them.

"My mother was pivotal in my finding my niche in music. She made it very clear early on that I would be involved in extra-curricular activities so that I wouldn't have time to get involved with the wrong crowd. That would have been easy to do while living in Camden, New Jersey. My father helped me cultivate that love for music and to this day, we bond over our love of jazz music."

Carlyle had some final thoughts that he wanted to share. "For those who live outside the law enforcement profession, there are police officers who intend to protect the public and serve honorably. We are the majority and exist in every city, town, neighborhood, community, and jurisdiction. We acknowledge that there are individual officers who do not deserve to wear the badge. In my opinion, no one despises a bad police officer more than a good police officer. There are improvements to the profession that can and should be made as well as to the overall criminal justice system. I remain hopeful that there will be productive conversations on ways to heal past traumas, address negative experiences, and discuss ways to improve police-community relationships. On a more personal note, if a police officer has never told you that you matter, this is for you—you matter, and we are in this together.

"For other police officers, an overwhelming majority of the public supports you and the work you do. I remember a college professor citing that not every community is at odds with its police department. We are expected to do a tough job with, at times, limited resources. Please maintain hope, optimism, and encouragement under difficult circumstances. I acknowledge the horrors you are exposed to daily; this is where the importance of self-care comes in. Please mind your mental health throughout your career. It is okay to talk and seek support. Please watch over your coworkers and trust those senses when you feel something may not be 'right' with one of them. It's okay not to be okay. In the face of adversity, I hope that we find healthy ways to cope and get support if needed. If no one has ever told you that you are appreciated, standby to copy: You are appreciated. We are in this together."

Carlyle, thank you for your service to your community.

Carlyle can be reached at criche@baltimorecountymd.gov.

FOUR

Deputy Chris Flores

Leon County Sheriff's Office (Florida): 2 Years
Florida A&M University Police Department: 2 years
Active Duty: 4 Years of Service

I spend time on social media, primarily focusing on both volumes of the *Behind and Beyond the Badge* books that I wrote. One of my goals is to humanize the badge and showcase the positive things that law enforcement officers and all first responders do every day. At times, I'll do a book giveaway or participate in a giveaway with another person or organization.

That's how I met Deputy Chris Flores. Chris had started following my Instagram account "behind and beyond the badge" and entered one of my book giveaways. I had no idea who Chris was, but he was selected as the winner by a random draw. When

I messaged him and asked where to ship the book, he provided a Tallahassee, Florida address—my hometown.

A conversation ensued, and he told me that he was a deputy at the Leon County Sheriff's Office (LCSO). This agency has 271 sworn deputies, 236 corrections officers, and 181 civilian employees. I shared that I was retired from the Tallahassee Police Department (TPD), and we discovered we had mutual friends in the profession.

After reading my books, Chris reached out and shared his thoughts with me. I always love when people take the time to do this. His comments were humbling but also made me smile as they reminded me of one of the reasons that I chose to write the books. Others who do the job felt as he did. He now knew that he was not alone in his thoughts as a law enforcement officer.

I follow both LCSO and TPD in our local news and on social media. A few months after meeting Deputy Flores, I was scrolling through the LCSO site and came across his name. They had posted about some awards they had recently presented. Deputy Flores had been selected as the Community Policing Deputy of the Year for 2021. After reading more about why Chris had been chosen, I knew I wanted him in this book. Once again, I reached out to him, and he agreed to let me tell his story.

We eventually found a date and time that worked for both of us, and I finally got to meet Chris in person. I loved everything about our conversation and getting to know him better. As with everyone in my books, I'm honored that he's trusted me to tell his story, and that I have a new friend and "brother in blue."

Chris grew up in Miami, Florida. After graduating from high school, he enlisted in the United States Air Force and served from 1998–2004. He was an avionics technician and worked on E3-B AWACS surveillance aircraft.

When I asked Chris why he chose to serve in the military, he responded, "We had no money for college, and everyone I knew at the time went to community college part-time and worked part-time but basically got nothing done full-time. I had to do more and also wanted to give back.

"My dad's family were political refugees fleeing Cuba and came to the United States with nothing. This country gave them a chance. We're all still very thankful. It's no coincidence I have a firefighter, a deputy, a paramedic-turned-nurse, another nurse, and multiple veterans in my family. I'm part of the first generation born here."

Chris spent the majority of his time stationed in Japan. He said, "The military afforded me the opportunity to travel, learn, lead, and serve during a difficult time in our country's history. I learned a lot of valuable lessons. As an example, in the military, there is no such thing as 'that's not my job.' All those lessons would help me later in life."

After leaving the military honorably as a staff sergeant, he moved to Tallahassee, Florida to be closer to his father and brother. He admits he had a tough transition back to civilian life.

"When I got out," he said, "I remember thinking that everyone's sense of humor was 'more sensitive' than what I was used to. I also had a difficult time working hard for someone else's profit margin. I had worked on important missions where the consequences were dire. Looking back, it was hard to find that motivation in a 'regular' job. Essentially, the service drove me to my current profession."

Everyone has a reason or a story as to how they chose a career in law enforcement. Chris brings a little different perspective. "Although I had been interested in law enforcement for a long time, it wasn't until the Michael Brown incident in 2014 and the ensuing riots that I decided to commit.

"I don't think anyone who hasn't applied for a law enforcement job can understand just how lengthy the application process is. It's certainly not a document you fill out and hope for the best. My goal then, as it is to this day, is to change people's perspective on law enforcement officers.

"We really are the sum of our experiences. I was raised to respect law enforcement, but the music I listened to during those years had an anti-police message. I also had some negative influences from older, more criminally inclined family members as well as from my own not-so-great interactions with the police.

"I saw cops as just cops, and that's it. I could relate to the store clerk or the office worker. I knew teachers had a life outside of work, but in my eyes, cops didn't. When I was in high school, the sister of some great friends of mine went to the academy and became a Metro-Dade police officer. I saw her in uniform every now and then but hung out with her and her coworkers while they were off duty.

"They turned out to be regular, flawed, relaxed people. My older brother, who I've always looked up to and perhaps inadvertently emulated, was also a law enforcement officer. He always talked about treating everyone with respect, from inmates to victims.

"I guess all of that prompted me to look into taking a Citizens Academy class offered by TPD. I remember Officer Tina Haddon was the coordinator. She and the other speakers explained why police officers did some of the things they did that I, as an uninformed civilian, had no idea about. I mean, how could I really have known?

"Most of my knowledge about law enforcement came from Hollywood movies and TV shows. Realizing how much I didn't know led me to later change my major in school from education to criminology. A few years later, I attended LCSO's Citizens Academy, where we learned about all the different specialty teams and the challenges law enforcement officers faced. They did a great job of humanizing the badge, and I was able to relate because of my time in the military.

"Later, when the news was vilifying cops and attempting to paint the people who do the job with a broad brush, I knew that wasn't accurate. Maybe I could do the job in a way that would hopefully leave a positive impression on people. In my opinion, law enforcement agencies don't do a great job of educating the public. In the meantime, people or organizations with questionable motives shine a bad light on and inaccurately portray the positive actions of the vast majority of law enforcement officers."

For a few years, Chris worked a variety of jobs and continued his education. He graduated from Florida State University in 2015, with a bachelor of science degree in criminology. Chris decided to apply for a police officer position at a local law enforcement agency and was hired. This agency sponsored (paid) him through the academy. Upon graduation, he began the field training officer program. Chris told me that he did well in the program advancing to the final two-week phase.

As a former field training officer and sergeant, sometimes things don't always work out for a variety of reasons. Chris decided to leave this agency and was hired by a smaller agency, The Florida Agricultural and Mechanical University (FAMU) Police Department.

He said, "It was a great experience because I really had to push myself just to make ends meet financially and had to think outside the box for training. I worked patrol and was a school resource officer.

"But there was a receptionist working 8:00 a.m.—5:00 p.m. who made more money than I did unless I worked overtime. One year, I worked 240 hours of overtime and many extra details. I was ready to give up being an officer, but I still wanted to be involved in law enforcement in some way. Luckily, Captain Jimmy Goodman, who is in charge of LCSO's Reserve Unit, and my brother convinced me to apply for a full-time deputy position. I'm so glad I did.

"I've now been with LCSO for two years and have worked in patrol. Currently, I'm a school resource deputy, tactical dive team member, team lead of Project 413, and the Explorer Program advisor and training coordinator. Finally, I'm at a place I love and want to be involved as much as possible."

Not all agencies have tactical dive teams or units, so I asked Chris to explain the purpose of having one, the process of getting on it, and why he wanted to be a part of it.

He responded, "I had been an active diver for years and wanted to learn a new aspect. Our dive team is a regional team that conducts underwater search and recovery work, not rescues. Anything from cars, guns, or other evidence that criminals may have disposed of in a body of water. At times, this can include human remains.

"While we do have some nice springs in North Florida, it's mostly rivers, retention ponds, lakes, and overall some nasty water where these activities take place. We are on call twenty-four hours a day, 365 days a year but do receive a monthly specialty team pay. Because only a few members can be on vacation at the same time, leave requests must be coordinated through the dive team commander.

"You need an open-water dive certification to apply for the team. Fortunately, I had many advanced certifications and over 1,000 dives prior to applying for this team. The tryout was held at a filthy, filthy pond at our regional academy. How filthy? Three showers later, I was still getting black muck out of my ears. Fortunately, none of my many dives involved water like this.

"The actual tryout involved wearing full equipment while running around the pond and a swimming and water-treading test without equipment. After that, the actual diving started. There was either zero or near-zero visibility. We had to follow a line underwater for some distance that included a few obstacles as well as conduct underwater dexterity and memory tests and search patterns. After those tests was an oral board.

"We train two days a month and are encouraged to dive recreationally on our off-duty time. The unit has two boats and a special truck used for gear. I had never backed trailers and driven boats, but they are a big part of this unit, and I'm still very new at that part. A lot of the equipment we utilize is not used in recreational or technical diving, such as full-face masks with the ability to communicate with those on land."

While Chris's path to where he is now wasn't the easiest, it was clear to me that he is passionate about his chosen profession and the people he serves. I believe his answer to the next question highlights what drives him and how it relates to all that he is involved with.

I asked him, "What do you feel is the most difficult part of your job?"

He answered, "Being vilified by loud voices in the media and, at times, within government and having people who have known you for years start believing what they hear from uninformed celebrities, talking heads, or professional athletes concerning law enforcement officers and the profession as a whole are the most difficult. I've already learned that election years can be rough, and during those times, contacts with the community are at times more negative.

"Then we go home, turn on the TV, check social media, or go to events, and the comments, opinions, and ignorance follow you. So what do we do? We stop hanging out with non-first-responder friends. We pull away. We spend our time trying to debunk ignorance instead of decompressing and taking care of ourselves. All of those things can take a huge toll."

So I asked Chris, "What do you personally do during your off-duty time to destress and rejuvenate?"

He said, "My number-one hobby is Brazilian jiu-jitsu. While I'm practicing it, my brain is 100 percent committed to it, but, when I'm done, I just feel calm. It also lets me connect with people who are not involved in law enforcement, and that's important to me.

"I strongly believe that there is nothing better an officer can do than learn a martial art. It can help you stay calm in an altercation and potentially reduce the amount of force used on a suspect. Plus, it's a lot of fun and something that you can involve your family in."

Many officers can share at least one thing that they would consider a career-defining moment. The situation that Chris describes is one that is often encountered by officers and highlights just how things are not always as they appear.

He said, "I had a call that involved an excited, out-of-control male. This guy was acting like some zombie monster out of a horror movie.

"He repeatedly bit and chomped on the rough asphalt, and it took five of us to pin him to the ground to control him, hoping that he wouldn't injure himself. I can still hear the sound that made. I turned his head to the side hoping that he would stop and not hurt himself, brushed the dirt off his face, and told him to breathe as we waited for emergency medical services to arrive.

"Everyone around was filming us and protesting that so many officers were on one guy. Once medication was administered, he was calm within seconds. Apparently, he had ingested acid that caused his behavior. The following week, I learned that this guy was a college student with no criminal history, just a regular kid who had made a poor choice. It reminded me that I usually meet people on their worst day, and often their behavior is not who they really are. I try to keep that in mind."

When people see these types of situations, they often jump to incorrect conclusions. For Chris, that's why those people who take the time to show their support are important to him.

He shared, "Kind words help keep me going. I am so thankful to the people who take the time and make the effort to give me a thumbs up or say something nice. There have been times when there is nothing but negativity toward cops on mainstream media and on social media. In those times especially, a show of support keeps me going. But the ones who really give me a boost are the ones who say they don't usually like cops, but you're okay. That's very much in line with one of the reasons I chose this profession.

"It's often a challenge, but I've learned to not take the insults personally. And sadly, I've also learned to disassociate with what terrible scenario I'm involved with. We're all human, but you have to turn the emotions off and get the job done."

One of Chris's favorite parts of the job is with the LCSO's Explorer Program. It's offered by many law enforcement agencies and teaches high school and college-aged students about law enforcement. Some Explorers go on to become officers themselves.

Chris said, "We expose them to different situations that are commonly faced by law enforcement. They do volunteer work and compete in subject areas related to the profession. I tell them that after they spend time in the program that they will know more about law enforcement than the majority of people they see talking as experts on the news. I'm happy to help any Explorer who wants to go to the academy and seek a career in law enforcement. However, I'm equally happy to see them become business owners, teachers, or whatever other profession they choose.

"We've had many great kids come through the program, but two really stand out for me. One was a young girl who was connected to me by a school counselor where I'm the resource deputy. She was struggling but is now heavily involved in the program and wants to become a law enforcement officer.

"Another kid comes from an immigrant family who was very distrustful of law enforcement. They all now have a different opinion, and he too wants to become an officer.

"I'm bilingual, which has helped not only on calls for service and as a school resource deputy, but I've also been able to help with some investigations. It has really been beneficial to be able to connect with Spanish speaking students. Many of them aren't used to seeing an officer who shares a similar background."

As a school resource deputy, Chris has the opportunity to work with kids in the education environment. He explained, "Most kids start the year off not liking me, but after a few months, they come to my office to vent and will often go out of their way to say hi to me. It's even better when it's a student I've arrested or given a civil citation to. Same thing goes with the parents. I've had them hug me and even bring me eggs from their farm.

"It takes a village to raise a child, and while my primary job is keeping students safe, I feel that I am 100 percent a part of that village, and they see that. Of course, sometimes things don't work out the way victims or even suspects want, but a small difference is still a difference. That's one of my goals!

"During the summer when school is out, I get to help out with other programs that involve kids. These programs have a positive impact on our youth and often changes their perception of law enforcement officers for the better.

"We need informed people, young and older, in our community. We need informed voters, and we need informed community partners. It's rewarding to help educate these young people who otherwise might only have a limited viewpoint. If the only people who have knowledge about law enforcement, work in law enforcement, we're failing."

Chris and I are passionate about mental health issues for law enforcement officers and all first responders. He has become involved with two entities that deal with those issues and hopes to become certified in crisis management.

The first organization is called the 2nd Alarm Project, a Tallahassee-based nonprofit that deals with first responder mental health and substance abuse. It is geared primarily toward the fire service, emergency medical services, and dispatcher professions and some law enforcement.

Chris is the law enforcement liaison. This group is heavily embedded in the Florida panhandle first responder community. They help agencies build peer support teams, train clinicians in the specific needs of first responders, and provide services.

He said, "Thanks to Dr. Kellie O'Dare Wilson, my longtime friend and director of the 2nd Alarm Project, I had developed an interest in first responder mental health. Couple that with the events and unrest during the summer of 2020 and my own past experiences, I recognized that first responders aren't necessarily keen on talking to a mental health professional.

"I fully understood why. Would it hurt my career, or could I possibly lose my job? Could it conceivably be used in some negative way against me? The concept of peer support really seemed like something that might actually work in this community. I was excited about the possibility of having that as a resource here. It is because of this hope that I first became involved with LCSO's Project 413, our peer support initiative.

"I contacted Nicole Troestrup, our wellness coordinator, during her first week of work at LCSO. After introducing myself, I offered any help I could provide. I was also contacting other agencies and learning as much as I could about the wellness and peer support concepts.

"I was working on it right up to the time I went on vacation during spring break of 2021. While I was away, a friend and former shift mate called around midnight to tell me that one of our own, someone I knew, had taken their own life.

"I thought that because I had spent so much time recently learning about law enforcement suicide, I would be at least somewhat prepared, but I wasn't. I guess deep down, I never thought it would happen here. And not to someone I knew. I thought I knew what a suicidal person looked and acted like, but I didn't.

"I didn't know this deputy well and had only worked a few shifts with them. I was hundreds of miles away on vacation, but I started checking on people. Some cried, some were just angry, all of them blamed themselves. I just listened.

"Out of this incident, Project 413, LCSO's peer support initiative, was created. It is a group of volunteers that represent all levels of rank and experience including retirees. Florida statute 111.09, peer support for first responders, even recognizes and outlines peers and their responsibilities.

"My coworker and friend began telling me about a three-year-old who swallowed a watch battery and his experience as the first officer on the scene. It was horrific, and he remembered every single detail. He finished by saying, "That was three years ago, and I've never told that to anyone."

"Imagine having to respond to another call right after that one. Yet officers are required to do just that. And three years ago? And as a father of small children? That adds up."

"Project 413 sounds formal, but for me, it really is just about changing the culture, that we don't have to pretend we're super tough and nothing affects us. That means we can talk and even joke about a call during our shift or on our off time, that we can discuss our thoughts and get it off our chest before going home.

Chris has received two awards—FAMUPD Rookie of the Year and LCSO Community Policing Deputy of the Year (2021).

In reference to the last award, Chris explained, "I didn't do anything other deputies don't do on a regular basis. My supervisor at the time was great at documenting all the things I'm involved with. The award mentioned a blanket drive that I started. I actually did the easy part, which was collecting items and handing them out to homeless citizens as I encountered them on patrol during the winter of 2020.

"My friends, who are former deputies, did the social media leg work and collected most of it. With the help of neighbors and friends, what began as a blanket drive turned into a food, socks, toothbrush, jacket, and blanket drive. I wish the people who helped could have seen the gratitude on the recipients' faces when my shift-mates and I were able to distribute them. I have a hard time speaking about this because it honestly pales in comparison to the acts of kindness that I've seen other deputies routinely do."

When asking people to be part of one of my books, I'm always curious why they agree to do it. But not everyone who is asked chooses to participate, and I'm okay with that.

Chris answered, "I loved your first two books because they focused on the person. Their frustrations and passions came through. Having met some of the people featured, reading their stories let me get to know who they are, not just what they do for a living. I hope readers will understand that first responders are just regular people like them who've, for a variety of reasons, chosen to do a difficult job."

Chris is married and told me that he has a very supportive family. He added, "Without them and their understanding, I don't think I would be able to do this job. The weeks when you work every day and every evening, the missed celebrations, the missed special occasions, and the postponed holidays take some getting used to. However, the worry they feel when you don't check in during your shift or come home on time is something I do not envy. I've realized the job will be gone one day, but family will be there long after if you make them a priority."

I always ask everyone if they have any thoughts in general that they'd like to share.

Chris responded, "To other law enforcement officers, thank you for what you have already done and choose to continue to do. If at some point you feel you must walk away from the career, do so. Maybe you'll come back to it rejuvenated, or maybe you'll find another way to contribute; there are plenty of ways. If you stay doing something you no longer like or have a passion for, you'll come to resent it. Citizens will notice, and your family will notice.

"Enjoy your off time. We need balance. Get yourself a hobby, not something you "used to do" but something you look forward to and enjoy and actually do every single week.

"To the people outside of the law enforcement and first responder world, if an agency near you offers a Citizens Academy, please participate in it. You will have fun and learn so much. I've asked my friends in other states to do this as a personal favor to me.

"This job is difficult. Anything and everything could happen at any given time. When you have a better understanding of how and why we do things and give us your support, it makes a world of difference. A simple wave or head nod is appreciated."

Chris, thank you for your service to your country and to your community.

FIVE

Deputy Chief of Police, Major Jim Russell

Florida State University Police Department (Florida)
Retired: 25 Years of Service

I have known Jim for many years. While we worked at different agencies, our paths crossed at community events that required manpower from many of our local agencies. Florida State University (FSU) home football games are one of those events. Jim had his assignments and responsibilities for the FSUPD, and I had mine for the Tallahassee Police Department (TPD), but we often saw each other at the pre-event briefings.

I've admired Jim for many years, not just for his wonderful career, but also for his willingness to always open his heart and speak freely. When I decided to write this book, I knew that I wanted to tell his story. I reached out, and he quickly said yes.

Jim is one of those individuals who had initially chosen a different course of study in college that didn't include becoming a law enforcement officer. He said, "I actually started college with the intent of graduating as a fine artist. As I progressed through the curriculum, I became aware that there just may not be many opportunities to make a living from creating art. I began to think about expanding my horizons. As it happened, my brother-in-law Brian LaVigne had recently started his career in law enforcement with the Largo Police Department in Largo, Florida.

"While I was home from college for the summer, Brian asked me if I wanted to do a ride-along. I thought why not and went down to see what his job was all about. Well, suffice it to say, I found the experience exciting and engaging. It sparked the idea that if Brian could do this, then why not me?

"When I got back home from my little trip to experience police patrol, my mom asked me what I thought about it. My response was "I loved it!" My mom's response wasn't quite as enthusiastic. I had always thought police stuff was cool but just never really thought about doing it. Now, I was fully focused on law enforcement as a career and promptly changed my college major from fine arts to criminology. I graduated from FSU in 1991 with a bachelor of science in criminology.

"Of course, that didn't mean that I was giving up art. In fact, I saw a law enforcement career as a real-world augmentation of the core drive behind my art. I was an activist who wanted to contribute to making things better, and law enforcement had revealed itself as one of the most direct ways to do this. For me, art would become a side gig, and I would keep the iron hot so that I could pick it up anytime when I was ready to do so."

While attending the law enforcement academy at Seminole State College, Jim also worked as a receptionist at his sister

Cyndie's hair salon. In his off time, he was actively seeking a job in law enforcement. One of the agencies that he had applied to was FSUPD. How Jim found out that he'd been hired by FSUPD still makes him smile. He shared with me the story.

"While working at the salon one day," he started, "I got a call from FSUPD's office administrator. She asked when I might be available to be measured for a ballistic vest.

"This seemed weird to me because I hadn't heard anything since my last interview with them. I asked her, 'Uh, does this mean I'm hired?'

"She was a little taken aback and said, 'What? Nobody told you? Yes, you're hired!'

"Kind of important to tell new hires that they are, in fact, hired!"

Jim graduated from the academy in December 1992 and started working for the FSUPD in February 1993. He served in many different roles, including patrol officer, field training officer (FTO), and crime prevention officer. He rose through the ranks and retired in 2018 as the deputy chief of police.

When asked what his favorite assignment was, he didn't hesitate to respond. "This is easy. I enjoyed myself the most as an FTO on patrol. I liked being connected and engaged with the community while helping new officers cut their teeth. I remember when people would ask me one of the reasons I liked law enforcement, I'd often tell them that I could not see myself in a job behind a desk. As I found out, getting promoted for doing a good job often lands you right where you don't want to be—behind a desk."

Even though FSUPD is a smaller agency, it's in Florida, which means having a plan in place to deal with hurricanes. But as an institution of higher learning, it also means being prepared for just about anything, especially active shooter scenarios. Jim was very involved with this aspect and shared, "I was often deeply involved in disaster response and preparation. As a command-level officer and a public information officer (PIO), much of my training and interaction was based on media outreach, community alerts, and community education.

"I was on the team that developed and implemented the FSU Alert Notification System, which is active to this day. This application had the ability to quickly notify students, faculty, staff, other emergency agencies, and the media of developing threats on and near the campus. I was one of just a few employees who was authorized to send emergency messages without prior approval when the circumstances called for it. This responsibility put me in very close working relationships with FSU, state, local, and federal emergency management entities. More than once, I was the Emergency Operations Center Incident Commander at FSU when the police chief was not available.

"FSUPD was very engaged and prepared to deal with large scale emergencies. They ensured that staff was highly skilled in incident command, National Incident Management System (NIMS), active shooter response, and multi-threat incident response. In fact, the department would eventually be a go-to agency to train smaller agencies in incident command and disaster response.

"Personally, I have responded in some capacity to many disastrous incidents, including hurricanes, tropical storms, campus fires, and of course, an active shooter situation. Later on in my career, my involvement would normally be to ensure an FSU Alert was sent and then follow up with media as well as briefing FSU senior staff. At this time, I was also in command of staff over the Support Services and Operations sections, so oversight of critical response functions was a major piece of my job, and I was fortunate to have very competent staff."

Jim mentioned active shooter response. No agency ever wants to put to use this type of training, but these scenarios have become more prevalent in today's society. The mindset of law enforcement has shifted from *what if* to *when* one of these incidents happens in their community. Sadly, this did happen on the FSU campus.

Jim explained what occurred. "On November 20, 2014, at about 12:30 a.m., a subject entered the Strozier Library on campus and started shooting. He was a deeply disturbed individual who had recorded a video saying that he felt he was being mentally tormented by the government, and the only way to call attention to his plight was to create a deadly and shocking incident.

"As the subject approached the library, he shot one student, leaving him critically injured and permanently paralyzed. Just inside the building, he shot another student in the leg and had, at some point, shot another student who escaped injury via a well-loaded backpack.

"As calls poured in to the 911 center and FSUPD, officers immediately rushed to the library. This included five FSUPD officers and one Tallahassee Police Department officer who happened to be nearby. As they arrived, the subject's pistol jammed, but he cleared it and walked outside. He found himself within a semicircle of guns-drawn officers, all who had arrived on scene in less than one minute.

"They shouted for him to drop the gun while he pointed it at himself and wildly yelled about defying compliance. Finally, he pointed his firearm in the direction of an officer and pulled the trigger. The subject died in a storm of gunfire with officers hitting their target twenty-six times.

"Of course, a full after-incident investigation took place, which resulted in the officers' actions being upheld by a grand jury. Sadly, the subject's actions and death were an indictment of our mental health system's inability to protect him from his own actions. His story was and is a tragedy.

"As with many major incidents, my role was to respond as the PIO, support the chief and other departments, and also ensure that FSUPD was geared to support all subsequent follow-up investigations. The Tallahassee Police Department and the Florida Department of Law Enforcement conducted the criminal incident follow-up as FSUPD and the campus itself was not in the position to investigate, not only ethically, but also mentally.

"The shooting affected the involved officers greatly, and not all of them recovered quickly from it. Being involved in a deadly shooting is traumatic enough, but this case didn't simply involve a criminal, but rather somebody who was disconnected from reality and likely did not understand that help was available or might have been effective for him. While undoubtedly lives were saved by the officers' actions, it remains unfortunate that the subject lost his life essentially due to a severe mental illness.

"All of the officers continued in their capacity at FSUPD, and all were offered, and some took advantage of, follow-up mental health care. One officer in particular struggled with the weight of his decision to open fire. However, due to proper peer and professional support, he continues his successful career in law enforcement to this day.

"The overall response by FSU as a community was incredible. Students, faculty, and staff came together to support one another, and as a group, they decided that as soon as they could, they would ensure the library was open for the pursuit of study. It was symbolic that from tragedy, the University would not be swayed from its mission and purpose. The support and thanks that came to the FSUPD was overwhelming to include the heroic actions of not only the officers, but also the dispatchers and nonsworn staff who sprang into action under the most dire of circumstances."

While the stories I write are focused more on the person behind the badge, individual incidents often affect and become a part of these people. Jim described a particular scenario that for him was one of those events. "I believe a key defining moment for me was July 30, 1999, when one of our officers, Chris Lee, was shot at the Tallahassee Memorial Hospital.

"I was actually working as a crime prevention officer at the time and was aware that our patrol officers had just arrested a suspect for check fraud at a college bookstore near campus. The suspect was huge by any standards and was pure muscle. Immediately after being arrested, the suspect began to complain of medical distress, so we had two officers, Chris Lee and John Wainwright, transport him to the hospital to be evaluated.

"Simultaneously, I was on-scene gathering information at a nearby fraternity house where the same suspect was possibly involved in the sexual battery of a female college student. When I finished there, it was time for me to head back to the station to get ready to go home for the day.

"Then, the radio exploded with Officer Lee screaming '10-24' (officer needs assistance) and that he had been shot.

"Apparently, after the suspect had been medically cleared to go to jail, Officer Wainwright left the emergency room to get the parked patrol car so that they could transport the suspect to the jail. At this time, the suspect attacked Officer Lee and literally ripped his gun out of the security holster. He pointed it at Officer Lee and told him to run. Officer Lee was not going to leave a gunman loose in a hospital emergency room, so he engaged the suspect, and a fight over the gun began. At one point, the suspect was able to point the gun back at Lee and pulled the trigger, sending a bullet through Lee's left arm and into his chest.

"Officer Wainwright heard the gunfire and rushed back to the emergency room. He couldn't make entry as the doors had been locked per hospital protocol. However, he and the suspect did exchange gunfire through the small window on the door. This was enough to cause the suspect to barricade himself in a small restroom.

"I remember when I heard Lee's call for help, it felt like electricity surged through my body. Another officer who had been chatting with me just about pulled the door off the cruiser to get in. Without any hesitation, we were on our way to the hospital with blue lights flashing and the siren blaring.

"With the assistance of just about every law enforcement agency in the area, the suspect remained pinned down in the bathroom. When he realized escape was impossible, he shot himself in the head and died from his injuries.

"This incident has affected me ever since, perhaps even being the source of a long battle with anxiety. But in another way, I was able to see for myself that under the worst of situations, such as an officer under fire, I would rush to the scene without hesitation. It was a good thing to know for myself that I would do what needed to be done.

"As for Chris Lee, he fully recovered from his wounds and received a Medal of Valor from the FSUPD. Yet his loving colleagues gave him a very heartfelt gift that maybe he liked a little more—a T-shirt with a big round target on it that said, 'I got shot and all I got was this lousy T-shirt!'"

At the time this incident occurred, I was the sergeant supervising TPD's Homicide Unit. We were tasked with conducting the investigation and preparing the presentation to the grand jury.

While I recall the incident, I had forgotten that Jim had respond-ed to the hospital. It was truly a chaotic scene and an incident that deeply affected not only law enforcement personnel but also the hospital and emergency room staff.

When talking about law enforcement officers and the job it-self, Jim will often mention the emotional impact it has on peo-ple. He's keenly aware of and a huge proponent of mental health awareness, not just for law enforcement officers but for all first re-sponders. There were several reasons why I asked Jim to let me tell his story, but one is that he is very open about his own mental health struggles and is always willing to share his thoughts.

He said, "I went for many years dealing with depression, likely starting when I was in my late teens. I remember that there would be times when I would start to go down a very dark place of de-spair. As I aged and went through college, I had no idea why.

It wasn't until my early years in law enforcement that I was actually struggling with a mental illness.

"Left untreated, what would sometimes be a day or two of depression would over time become weeks of misery and being in a very hopeless mental state. As I continued doing art on the side during my law enforcement career, some of my work would reflect my mental state. I tried to express how I was feeling in my painting, and the resulting artwork would often appear, as a friend put it, shocking.

"While a developing case of major depressive disorder (MDD) would normally be enough to challenge anyone, add onto this the daily stress of law enforcement, and depression was taken to a whole other level. Even more so, due to the job itself, I was developing anxiety as well. I was declining fast. My mar-riage began to dissolve as I pushed away loved ones. I didn't know then, but I know now, that a symptom of depression is self-isolation. It's not because depression makes one hate others, but rather, depression tells you that you are unworthy of love, attention, and friendship by others. You just want to be left alone in a cave.

"It doesn't get better if left alone. It gets worse. As my marriage came apart, so did my ability to cope with the feelings I had. They are very hard to describe. For long and intense periods of time, I felt worthless, like a burden, isolated, unloved, and so down that I became emotionally numb. I didn't want to be here anymore, and I was having serious suicidal ideations including how, when, and where I would end my life.

"Importantly, one must understand that when you are talking about suicide, the impulses and drives leading up to an attempt are not rational. My thoughts were not rational. In fact, as I now know, many people loved and respected me. By all appearances, I was doing great at work and quickly on my way up. But I was good at covering up the war inside my head. I was in very serious trouble, but then somehow, luck smiled on me.

"I was having a meeting at FSU with a world-renowned suicidologist who was assisting me, ironically, on the development of a suicide prevention program for officers and other members of the FSU community. In separate incidents a couple of weeks apart, two students had killed themselves in the same residence hall.

"The university was motivated to develop and implement additional programs as soon as possible. As my campus colleague conveyed to me his input on things to look out for as far as symptoms of impending suicide, I realized he was describing me perfectly. A light bulb went on in my head, and I recognized that what was happening to me was real, and, moreover, there was help. I kept my cool during the meeting, but at the first opportunity, I set up an appointment with my family doctor.

"It didn't take long for me to get a diagnosis of depression. I was placed on medication and referred to therapy. It helped tremendously. Once the medication brought some hope back to life, I looked back and couldn't believe I had been suffering unnecessarily for years and years. However, I had another step that I needed to take. I needed to tell my boss, the chief of police.

"I really didn't know what to expect. Perhaps the chief might support me, but what about his bosses? What if the president of the university was not comfortable with FSUPD's second-in-command having mental health issues? I knew I had to disclose to the chief my struggle, but I also knew it just might mean the end of my career.

"It was February 2010, and I told him everything, even that I had been suicidal. Chief David Perry paused and thought a moment before saying, "Well, Jim, whatever you need, we've got your back, and we'll support you. Now shouldn't we get back to work?"

"I couldn't have asked for a better response. In that short reply, the chief told me that not only could I count on support, but also that he trusted me with the job. I knew that while I was not responsible for having depression, I was responsible for managing it and doing a good job. I was determined not to let the chief down.

"As I learned more about depression and mental health challenges facing first responders, I realized that if it could happen to me, and nobody knew about it, then it could certainly be happening to others, including officers in my department. I decided that I would not combat mental health affliction just for me but also for other officers and employees.

"In 2012, at an all-hands-on-deck meeting, I told the entire agency my story and told them that FSU would support any of them who were struggling with mental health. I wasn't sure what the reaction would be or if I would find myself issued a rubber gun. I quickly learned that in addition to my agency as a whole embracing me, several officers came up to me after the meeting and thanked me for what I said. Several have since gotten help for themselves and/or family members.

"It is vitally important that law enforcement agencies create a "culture of permission" for asking for help when it comes to mental health. Too often, we are focused on being the ones who are always in control and taking charge, but when our brains get an illness, we do not have the tools or know the resources about what to do. The top administrators at departments need to be very clear and vocal to staff that there is help, help is encouraged, and employees will not be punished or ridiculed for seeking help.

"If we really love our fellow law enforcement officers, that's the right thing to do," he added.

Jim went on to say that chasing the bad guys wasn't the most difficult part of the job. Instead, it was the constant feeling of stress and anxiety under the surface. It's especially difficult for those in a position of being on-call twenty-four hours a day like he was. He felt that there was no real system in place to allow him to actually disconnect from work.

He said, "Mentally, this disallowed any true respite from work, and over time, sowed the seeds of seeking retirement as soon as feasible. This can also be an example of how intrusive work can be in personal lives and the damage that it can do mentally."

Jim loved his job and profession despite the stress. Physical fitness activities were always important to him, and he focused on weightlifting, specifically powerlifting. But as time went on, his knees decided that he needed to find a different outlet to stay physically fit.

He added, "What started as a means to lose a little weight and stay fit quickly developed into an obsession with cycling. My first goal was to ride a bike one-hundred miles in a single ride. Once I completed that, I just wanted to do another and another. I also sought out more challenging rides and began doing ultra-distance bike races.

"In 2005, in my first distance bike race in Sebring, Florida, I got a third-place medal riding 166 miles in twelve hours. While not a win, it showed me a clear path that I could race bikes and be successful. Bike rides that I completed over the years included rides of 100, 125, and 200 miles, and some that took twenty-four hours of straight riding.

"I organized bike rides for safety around the state of Florida. The first two rides were sponsored by Anheuser-Busch and the next three sponsored by GEICO. The longest of these was in 2007 for the 180 Energy Drink SAFE Ride where the team and I rode twelve-hundred miles in twelve days to promote traffic safety.

"One of the most challenging things I did was to be the crew chief for Team Kinema in the 2012 Race Across America (RAAM), widely known as the toughest ultra-endurance bicycle race in the world. Together with the crew, we ensured that a team of riders made it across the continent by bicycle in eight days, eighteen hours, and forty-eight minutes. At one point, I was awake for sixty hours straight before finally getting a few hours of sleep in the back of a Chevy Suburban in some mountains that I can't even remember where. This was the absolute hardest mental and physical task I ever had to do. Happily, the team won its age group!"

While touching on some of the negative aspects of the law enforcement profession, Jim is emphatic about what his favorite part of his work was. He shared, "I think the most fulfilling part of the job was the relationships that were created and continue to this day. Many of the journalists as well as citizens who I interacted with remain friends of mine to this day. I feel like I can be better friends with them now because I am no longer under the umbrella of being a cop.

"Being a cop is like being an actor and having to abide by a certain image. I'm no longer constrained by what I can and can't say, and the relationships I have are much more genuine. Interestingly enough, my strongest circle of friends are not law enforcement officers but people far outside the police world. I think this is healthy and has provided me many more options for growth and happiness."

With a career spanning twenty-five years, Jim easily recalled the nicest compliment he had received. "It wasn't so much as a compliment but an action. I don't recall the exact year but possibly 1996. I was serving as an Adopt-A-COP at a residence hall at FSU. The Adopt-A-COP Program was essentially a community-oriented policing program where patrol officers would be 'adopted' by a residence hall. The officers would conduct extra patrols of their particular residence hall, do crime prevention presentations and programs, and in general, interact with the residents.

"One evening, we got a call that a resident wanted to report that she was sexually assaulted by another student. She told our dispatch that she only wanted to talk to her Adopt-A-COP, Officer Russell. This has always stuck with me that the level of trust was there to specifically ask for me to investigate the incident. To this day, I hate that this happened to her, but it was an honor to serve her in one of the scariest and most painful times of her life. If I remember correctly, we got the guy who did it too."

Jim and I talked about what he felt was the most important quality to have to be a good law enforcement officer. His comments were a bit different than many. He said, "I think the best cops are the ones who realize that their entire persona is not, and I believe shouldn't be, wrapped up in a job. To be a good law enforcement officer, one must be humble and understand that they are part of the community and not an overseer. They must have the mental understanding that they represent their neighbors as one of them. It keeps them balanced and better equipped to interact with fellow citizens in a positive way."

In 2018, Jim decided to retire and move on to phase two of his life. He has gone back to his love of art and opened an art studio. He told me, "I have always loved art. In fact, it was my first career choice, but unless one lands a dream job, it's a very unstable career choice. When I was ready to retire, and after twenty-five years I was ready, I crunched the numbers and found that I could actually pursue my art dreams and not starve.

"There is nothing I do halfway, so when I decided to dive into art, I did it with the full intention of being a professional artist and making a living at it. During my law enforcement career, I might do four or five paintings a year. Now as a full-time professional artist, I am doing four or five paintings a week. It is a completely different scenario than law enforcement, but I love doing what I enjoy doing and not having to maintain an official persona, which was never really me anyway.

"The idea to move my workspace out of my home and into Railroad Square was a pure business decision. As an art hub of the Tallahassee community with regular events occurring, it made perfect sense to set up and do work at the park. I certainly like creating in a supportive community, and as a bonus, my house is not overflowing with paintings!"

I have visited Jim at his studio several times, and his talent constantly amazes me. While he paints whatever he wants, he also does commissioned pieces. Some of those that I've seen are phenomenal works of art. I am definitely not a professional art critic, but I think I love his work because I know it comes from his heart and that he's proof that there is life after a career in law enforcement!

Besides his art, Jim is still active in his community. He currently serves on the board of directors for The Community Thrift Market in Support of Tallahassee Action Grants, Inc. This organization awards grants to nonprofit entities doing work in our community. He is also a speaker with We Save Lives, a traffic safety organization focused on reducing drunk, drugged, and distracted driving.

He and his wife Connie are contributors to the Matthew Beard Award for Excellence in Research, which supports promising up-and-coming researchers pursuing their work at the FSU Marine Lab.

I asked Jim why he chose these particular causes, and he explained. "I have always been concerned about driving under the influence (DUI) in our community. Before I met Connie, I was very involved, also serving as the Chair of the Leon County Multi-Agency DUI Strike Force. I met Connie at a candlelight memorial vigil on the FSU campus in January 2007. This was a few weeks after her son Matthew was killed by a drunk driver in South Florida.

"Matthew was an aspiring marine biologist at FSU on his way to a dive during Christmas break. While stopped in traffic on I-95, the car Matt was riding in was struck from behind by a DUI driver at ninety miles per hour. Matt sustained a catastrophic brain stem injury and died after being in a coma for eight days with his mother by his side.

"Connie became a passionate activist for the prevention of DUI, and we began working together on DUI programming. We became friends. On the day my divorce was final, she asked me out. A little over a year later, we were married. We have since continued to work together to get the word out about DUI and have most recently spoken to members of the USAF at Eglin Air Force Base."

Having settled into his retirement life away from law enforcement, an unexpected and tragic event rocked his family's world. This is a formal explanation of what occurred:

"On January 11, 2021, at about 11:00 p.m., Master Corporal Brian LaVigne was one shift away from finishing a near thirty-two years in law enforcement, thirty of which were with the Hillsborough County Sheriff's Office.

"He dedicated every day to his family, community, and fellow deputies, even just a day before he was to turn in his gear and enjoy a well-deserved retirement. He was a worker. As deputies pursued a suspect who had just assaulted two officers during a disturbance call, Brian, while not a direct part of the pursuit, set up his patrol car near an intersection ahead of the suspect's route, yet out of the way.

"As the suspect approached, he deliberately veered his car toward Brian's marked patrol car and slammed into the driver's side. Despite the desperate and heroic efforts of law enforcement and firefighters, Brian did not survive his injuries."

Master Corporal Brian LaVigne was Jim's brother-in-law. Jim said, "The impact on the family was and is devastating. A large emotional toll has been the shock and almost unbelievable, ridiculous, and unfairness of it all. A common term heard in the family was, "I just can't believe it" or "This is just fucking stupid." Brian was about to finally enjoy more of life with his family, who he put before anyone else. And as the universe would have it, he was struck down.

"Brian was my mentor. He was THE reason I got into law enforcement. I always looked up to him for his steadfast courage, moral bearing, dedication, and sense of right and wrong. He was not only a cop's cop, but he was also an example to everyone in his community.

"I still haven't fully absorbed his loss, but in a moment of grief, when I finally broke down after his funeral, I was angry with him. I yelled at him, 'Brian! You know better than to go out on patrol right before you retire! This is what happens!'

"I sobbed, angry, outraged, and unbelievably sad. In the moment, I had to talk to him and scold him for tempting the universe. Naturally, I know this was all emotions. Of course, Brian would go out for one more patrol shift. That is who he was, a committed cop every second he put on the badge. He would never be someone to avoid action, retirement imminent or not."

With that event still fresh and all that Jim is involved in, I hesitated to ask him about letting me tell his story. But I believed he had so much to share. When I reached out, he didn't hesitate to participate.

I asked Jim what he hoped people would garner from my books. He answered, "Law enforcement is too often portrayed as devoid of normal human traits, and I think educating the public is important. I also feel that active and retired law enforcement officers need to see that their personal stories are relatable to the experiences of others. To hear from those who have 'been there' may help light a path toward more success in their careers and personal lives. We learn through shared experiences, and frankly, in this field, we don't openly share our experiences enough. I hope this series continues to help our brothers and sisters feel less isolated and more apt to seek support when needed."

For Jim, his family was a major reason why he retired when he did. He explained, "They missed countless weekends and holidays with me. Even when we could get away, we really couldn't disconnect because I always had the department phone with me. Of course, it would always ring at some point with some crisis on the other end.

"I decided that to retire was to put them first. As I move forward with making the art career work, they have continued to be in my corner and support my artist goals. This can mean my spending long hours at the studio. But the good part is that when I want to be off, I can be off, and when I don't want to talk on the phone, I don't have to.

"So to Connie and my son Grayson, thanks for making everything worth it!" he stated.

As the final part of Jim's story, I asked him if there was anything that he wanted to share with the public in general or to those in law enforcement.

He responded, "I'll paraphrase the words of my sister Cathy, Brian's widow. She has recently said that it is important to remember that law enforcement is a job. While we do like to elevate our career to the level of 'a calling,' it is important to keep it in its place. As in any job, we can be replaced and forgotten quickly, but our family, true friends, and personal wellbeing are the most important things to attend to. Keep your priorities where they need to be because they are the ones that last and the ones that matter."

Jim, thank you for your service to your community and your willingness to open your heart and share.

Jim can be reached through his website: https://jimrussellart.com

*Photo by Katie Clark

SIX

Sergeant Eric McCants

Burke County Sheriff's Office (Georgia): 5 Years
Richmond County Board of Education: 1 Year
Paine College Police Department: 2 Years
Waynesboro Police Department: 1 year
Active Duty: 9 Years of Service

A few months ago, I was on LinkedIn and reading posts created by friends and colleagues. I started noticing posts created by Eric and reading comments that he had written. They were always positive and encouraging, and I began clicking on the "like" button for some of them. Not long after, Eric reached out to me asking to connect. I accepted, and we messaged several times.

I began to pay more attention to Eric's posts and realized that he lived and worked in Georgia, my neighboring state. But I didn't know anything about Burke County or where it was located, so I did some research.

Burke County is the second-largest county by area in Georgia but is small in population. According to the U.S. Census Bureau, its population in 2020 was 24,596. It sits on the eastern border of Georgia and western border of South Carolina.

The Burke County Sheriff's Office is the primary law enforcement agency in the county and has approximately 130 total employees. When I looked at their website, I read the "Sheriff's Message" written by Sheriff Alfonzo Williams. Simply put, I liked it. One statement in particular stood out: "Anyone who has worked with me knows I firmly believe in loyalty to the mission, not me!" Perusing the website, it's clear that Sheriff Williams also believes in being active with and within the community.

I reached out to Eric and told him about my *Behind and Beyond the Badge* book series, what they were about, and their intended message. This was followed by my asking him if he would let me tell his story. He requested some additional information, and an email was sent with much greater detail and what this would involve on his part. Eric agreed to participate.

One of the first questions I ask people is why they chose the law enforcement profession. I get a myriad of answers.

Eric responded by saying, "I honestly didn't choose law enforcement. Initially, I enrolled at Augusta State University with the intent of majoring in business management. My plan was to get my degree and then help my cousin Abia Williams grow his karate school.

"He had a pretty successful martial arts school, and I was his understudy. I spent hours training there and learning all the business aspects of the school. He was such a positive influence on me. But I was seventeen years old when I started at the university, and honestly, it was just too much for me. Attending class was secondary to socializing and partying. My grades suffered and I withdrew from school.

"I then went to work at a local grocery store. One day I over-heard a conversation between an officer working special security duty at the store and another young man. The officer told him about the academy and how amazing working in law enforce-ment was.

"My mother, as with most mothers, had been telling me that I needed to get back into school or find a different career path other than working at the store. She was a hard-working woman who raised my siblings and me as a single mother. School was important to her and she pushed us hard academically.

"Mom also made sure that we were deeply involved with music. Each of my siblings were involved in different orches-tras at the Augusta State University Conservatory Program. My brother played the violin and viola, and my sister played the cel-lo. I played the violin as well but eventually switched to trumpet.

"The thought of a career in law enforcement intrigued me, and I also saw it as a path that might keep my mother from hound-ing me! I entered the Augusta Technical College Law Enforce-ment Academy in January of 2011 and graduated that June."

One of Eric's academy instructors, Alfonzo Williams, left the academy to accept the chief of police position at the Waynesboro Police Department. A few weeks before Eric graduated, Chief Williams offered Eric a police officer position at the department, which he happily accepted.

He said, "Looking back, the Waynesboro Police Depart-ment was a great agency to work for with a lot of amazing offi-cers, but I was just twenty years old. I really hadn't grown up, and in reference to my personal life, not much had changed.

Socializing and partying off-duty once again wasn't the best path. In December 2012, eighteen months after being hired, I was asked to resign."

A new police department in the area had been formed, the Paine College Police Department. The inaugural police chief was a lieutenant that Eric had worked with at the Waynesboro Police Department. After only a few months out of law enforcement, Chief Joseph Nelson offered Eric a job and another chance.

Eric explained, "Working on a college campus as an officer was a little different for me, different than working out in a larger community. As officers, we were a little more lenient with the students, and it took some time to adjust.

"Chief Williams and another mentor, Charles Prescott, had always emphasized how important it was for me to get my college education. While working at Paine College Police Department, I took their advice and once again enrolled in college."

Eric stayed at the Paine College Police Department until July 2015. At that time, Chief Williams was the police chief at the Richmond County Board of Education Police Department and offered Eric a job. He accepted the position as a school resource officer.

Eric shared, "I enjoyed working with the officers at Richmond County, but honestly, I wasn't a big fan of working with kids. I believe it takes a person with a tremendous amount of patience, and at that time, that wasn't my strong suit."

In 2016, Chief Williams entered the political race for the Burke County Sheriff's position and won the election becoming Sheriff Williams. Eric left the Richmond County Board of Education Police Department, and in January 2017, began working at the Burke County Sheriff's Office where he is today.

Eric's first position with the sheriff's office was as a road patrol deputy answering calls for service throughout the county. He also accomplished something that he is very proud of—graduating from the University of Phoenix with his bachelor of science degree in criminal justice administration.

While Eric enjoyed his time as a patrol deputy, he had his sights set on doing more. The department has a special unit called the Crime Suppression Team that handles special details targeting identified high-crime or crime-specific problems. This is where Eric wanted to be.

He started talking to the deputies assigned to this unit and on his days off, was allowed to work with them. His extra effort paid off, and he was selected to join the team.

Eric said, "I believe that I did my best work as a crime suppression deputy and made some of my biggest drug cases and arrests while on the team."

Things continued to move forward in a positive direction for Eric. While on the Crime Suppression Team, Eric attended a drug interdiction class and met Dennis Benigno. Dennis is the founder and CEO of Street Cop Training.

In his desire to become the best officer that he could be, Eric reflected, "I would spend hours talking with Dennis, asking questions, and sending him videos of my traffic stops so that he could critique them. I owe a lot of my success as an officer to him and the training that he provides."

Eric's passion to learn and always improve also fueled his desire to become a member of the department's Special Response Team (SRT), BCSO's name for their SWAT team. He knew this wouldn't be easy.

He explained, "I've always been a big guy, and I hated running. But I knew that I needed to get into better physical shape. I worked hard, lost fifty pounds, and finally made the team."

Sheriff Williams knew that Eric had obtained his bachelor's degree and encouraged him to pursue his master's. Eric again enrolled in the University of Phoenix, and in 2019, graduated with his masters of science degree in administration of justice and security. Once he completed school, the sheriff approached him about making some career changes.

Eric recalled, "Sheriff Williams thought that I had reached a point in my career where I should consider becoming a supervisor. I had worked hard on my education and training and had some valuable experience he felt I should share with others. This was not something that I initially wanted to do as I loved working on the Crime Suppression Team. But I listened, applied, and was promoted to sergeant.

"My first assignment as a sergeant was supervising a patrol squad on the night shift. It was an adjustment going from the suppression team back to handling calls for service on the road. I pride myself on being a hard worker and accepted the challenge in helping mold the younger and newer deputies on my squad. They had so much potential, and I tried to guide and encourage them to pursue a college education."

For all of his efforts, Eric was named the 2019 Special Operations Deputy of the Year.

After spending a year working the night shift, Eric was moved to the Narcotics Unit. Eric remains in that position and says that he's enjoying the learning process of long-term drug investigations.

With Eric's experience in different positions, I asked him what he believes has been the most difficult part of his job.

Without hesitation, Eric replied, "For me, it's seeing kids hurt or killed. As an officer, I've become emotionally numb when faced with a death scene. But when those scenes involve an innocent child losing their life, it just does something to me. It's hard to put into words.

"Just before Christmas last year, a call went out over the radio concerning a vehicle that was fully engulfed in flames with occupants trapped inside. When I arrived on the scene, it was total controlled chaos. Four people had been in the car—two adults and their two small children. One child was deceased on the scene, and the other had been transported to the hospital. So many different first responder agencies were there working together and doing their best. But sadly, not everyone always survives. Seeing that child dead on the ground, it's a mental picture that is with me almost daily."

But Eric also knows that the community is always watching and recording everything. He continued, "I just try to remember to be professional and calm in all situations. For me, patience is the most important quality that a good law enforcement officer should have. Sometimes I think that we as officers can forget that. Patience and understanding can go a long way in making situations and the people we come in contact with easier to deal with. I've had people tell me that a positive encounter with me has helped them choose a more positive life path.

"Those types of comments help remind me why I do this job. I also strive to give victims some sense of peace, whether it's capturing an offender or helping them in any way I can when dealing with a traumatic incident. These are the most fulfilling parts of my job."

I really admire Eric's ability to choose a goal and achieve it. It hasn't always been an easy path for him, but his dedication and drive keep moving him forward. He told me that in addition to Dennis Benigno, he has had some amazing mentors and instructors throughout his life and career and credits them with making him the law enforcement officer and man that he is today.

Eric talked openly about one particular individual who was involved in his life at an early age. "While we aren't related by blood, I always called Hirron Williams 'Uncle.' He took me under his wing and looked at me as his extra son. Hirron was an archbishop in our church, a master in martial arts, and a straightforward, no-nonsense man.

"His physical appearance stood out with his long dreadlocks and grey eyes. And when he walked into a room, most people would stop what they were doing. They could feel the energy that he possessed. He absolutely helped me become a better man."

All of those people who had a positive influence on Eric's life fueled his desire to become an instructor himself. He is now a certified instructor in the state of Georgia and recently taught his first class at the Augusta Technical Police Academy.

I mentioned at the beginning of Eric's story that I "met" him via LinkedIn. With over 25,000 followers, I asked him why he's so active on that site.

He stated, "LinkedIn has become a huge asset to me for several reasons. I've met some terrific individuals who've offered some incredibly useful and life-changing advice both personally and professionally. I post nothing but positive and encouraging things because I believe that's what we need to be doing.

"A coworker, Shedree Woods, introduced me to a book called *The Secret*. That book has helped me tremendously and continues to help me stay focused on what is important and not to worry about the negative things in life. There is so much negative in the world and people who continue to push the 'us versus them' agenda. I believe in a strong work ethic, staying positive, and encouraging others. It's my way of paying it forward.

"Mental health issues are a big concern for our profession, and I know we must do better. Perhaps in some small way, my presence on LinkedIn can help. I also want to help humanize the badge and hope that some of my posts do just that. We are all similar and struggle with the same things. Law enforcement officers have to wear so many different hats, and expectations of them are high. But most importantly, we are human."

Eric continues to have career goals and hopes that someday he'll become a state or federal agent. He wants the challenge of working long-term and complex cases. Another goal is to continue to improve and become the best instructor that he can be and help other officers grow their own skill set.

Staying active is a priority in Eric's life. He explained, "Going to the gym is something I enjoy doing on my off-duty time. I think of it as my emotional therapy, and certainly staying in shape helps with the job."

He is happily married to Latricia McCants. Together, they have five children, one girl and four boys.

He added, "Latricia was a calming influence on me when we met. She helps me stay focused and is so encouraging and supportive of my career goals."

Growing up, Eric said that his family was very close. His grandfather "Friggs" was the backbone that held them all together. Many of his fondest childhood memories are of his grandmother and grandfather laughing at and with each other. His grandfather was also a positive role model for him. When he died in 2015, Eric said, "a part of me left with him."

Family is still important to Eric and spending time with his wife and children is a welcomed priority. He enjoys going to the movies with the kids, playing video games with them, and just playing outside with them.

Eric knows that he often has to work late and sometimes on holidays, but his family has always been understanding and supportive of his career.

He also enjoys cooking. He shared, "My wife bought me a pellet grill, and it's been life-changing!"

Eric, thank you for your service to your community!

Eric can be reached on LinkedIn under Eric McCants or via the email address
mccants082002@gmail.com.

SEVEN

Sergeant Jason Harney

Las Vegas Metropolitan Police Department (Nevada)
Retired: Twenty-three and a half Years of Service

While looking for people whose stories I wanted in my book, saying I have "met" someone has now taken on a new meaning for me. With a goal of wanting to write about people who didn't live close to my home, it became logistically impossible to travel to meet everyone in person, not to mention a bit financially cumbersome. Then once you throw in travel restrictions created by the pandemic, I think you get the picture.

Jason is one of those people I "met" through social media and his film work. We've communicated on so many platforms but just haven't met in person. But I knew enough about him that I wanted to tell his story.

After graduating from high school in 1990, Jason joined the Nevada Army National Guard. He completed basic training and Military Police School at Fort McClellan, Alabama, in December of 1990. His plan was to begin classes in the spring semester at the University of Nevada, Las Vegas.

World events had a different plan when Iraq invaded Kuwait. Instead of going home after completing his training, he was sent to join his unit, the 72nd Military Police Company. The unit had been activated, and he was sent to Fort Ord, California, for pre-mobilization training and deployment. By late December, Jason and his unit were in Dhahran, Saudi Arabia, as part of the massive coalition forces that were there to liberate Kuwait through Operation Desert Shield.

After a short stay in Dhahran, Jason witnessed the official beginning of Desert Storm as Scud missiles were launched by Iraq. His unit's mission was to set up camp in the field where they performed the Enemy Prisoner of War Operations. As part of their daily duties, they transported, processed, housed, and guarded tens of thousands of Iraqi prisoners through June of 1991.

Five years later, Jason left the Nevada Army National Guard as a Sergeant E-5.

I ask everyone why they chose a career in law enforcement. Jason said, "The biggest influence in my choosing a law enforcement career was my father, Steve Harney, a retired Nevada Highway Patrol lieutenant. He had served from 1974 to 2004. I would not be where I am today, nor would I have had a successful law enforcement career if it were not for him. From a young age, he taught me the value and importance of setting goals, attention to detail, discipline, and giving your best effort in everything you do. Truth be told, I wanted to be an accountant in high school, but after returning home from Desert Storm, having now had the experience provided by the Army, there was no question what I wanted to do."

In June 1991, within weeks of returning home to Las Vegas, the Las Vegas Metropolitan Police Department (LVMPD) hired eighteen-year-old Jason as a police cadet. At the time, the police cadet position began with a six-week Corrections Academy, followed by one year of working in the Clark County Detention Center. Responsibilities included checking in inmate visitors and working in the property room where street clothes were collected and switched out for jail clothes. All of this was typically done alongside a corrections officer. For Jason, "It was a great experience in a controlled environment to begin learning about the criminal element."

Jason went on to add, "A year later, I moved to the next step as a police cadet. I attended an eight-week patrol academy and was then assigned to a substation and attached to a patrol squad.

"At the time, cadets would check out a patrol car with an "Out of Service" cover over the vehicle lights. We would then answer calls, such as report calls, where there would be no potential for suspect contact. As cadets, we continued this type of work until we turned twenty-one when we would then be sent to the next police academy class. I attended the LVMPD Police Academy, class 2/93, which ran from September, 1993 through January 1994.

His entire law enforcement career was spent with the LVMPD and included a variety of assignments. Jason was promoted to sergeant in 2002 and spent the final thirteen years of his career as a first-line supervisor with assignments as a patrol sergeant, academy sergeant, recruitment supervisor, and field training sergeant. When Jason retired, the LVMPD had approximately 5,800 total personnel, including 2,100 sworn police officers and 750 corrections officers.

In 1996, Jason became a defensive tactics instructor and said, "Because of my ongoing marital arts training background at the time, teaching defensive tactics quickly became my passion. Due to my dedication and proficiency in the topic, I was chosen to become a member of the academy staff just a year later."

In 2000, Jason left the academy and spent the next two years as a robbery detective. He was promoted to sergeant in 2002 and returned to the academy in 2005 as the academy sergeant to fuel his passion for training.

He said, "The time I spent both as a member of the academy staff and as the academy sergeant were some of the most rewarding of my career. We put through ten academies total, five classes as a member of the academy staff and another five classes as the academy sergeant. This included LVMPD's largest class ever, class 2/98. That class began with 125 recruits and 108 graduating. There was never a better feeling of accomplishment and satisfaction than watching a new class of police officers walking across the stage and receiving their badges, knowing what we as a staff had contributed to each one as they embarked on the next stage of their new careers. Over the course of two three-year assignments working at the LVMPD academy, we graduated over 750 officers."

When I ask people to recall the nicest compliment they had received from someone they helped, their response usually involves a particular incident. Jason's comments fell in line with his passion for teaching. "I'm sure there were a number of times I was a part of a solution to a situation on a call and helped someone in need. However, the compliments that resonate most with me were the ones I got after teaching a defensive tactics class, particularly the instructor courses.

"At eighty hours in length, the class gave an opportunity to really go in depth on a number of topics and techniques that many of the students hadn't received instruction on since graduating the academy years before. It was my responsibility to mold them into instructors capable of teaching at the squad level, thereby creating a higher level of proficiency throughout the department.

"At the end of any class I taught, whether at the academy, in service training, in instructor courses, or at squad level, the validation I always hoped to receive was that of an officer who felt their skill set was enhanced from my training. Every instructor within law enforcement will say the same. It's why training is our passion."

On a daily basis, police officers are forced to outwardly shut down their emotions to complete the task at hand. Everyone has their own way of becoming proficient at this. Jason shared his thoughts with me on this topic. "Confidence is also a crucial aspect of the work we do. I'm a firm believer in consistent training and experience leading an officer down a path that will ultimately result in the confidence needed to maintain a professional demeanor while handling a difficult incident.

"Everyone is wired differently, and there are a variety of factors in an officer's life that could influence how they handle different situations on an emotional level. As an example, let's say you find yourself on a call involving domestic abuse. It would be normal to have an elevated emotional response if you're married and make a connection between the circumstances of that call and your personal life.

"We are human beings after all, not robots. But nonetheless, there is a job to be done and certain expectations that must be met. We can reflect as a group after the call, something we always did in order to ensure everyone involved was okay."

I often ask people what they feel is the most important quality to have in order to be a good law enforcement officer. Knowing Jason's background, his answer didn't surprise me.

He said, "Professionalism is the most important attribute, but what does that actually mean? To me, it begins with ensuring you maintain what you have been taught in the police academy throughout your career. Those crucial life-saving skills can certainly erode over time, and it's up to us to ensure we continue to perform at an optimal level. Isn't that what the citizens we serve not only expect but deserve?

"This starts with your appearance. It's difficult to gain the respect of the public when you don't present a professional image. How an officer wears the uniform can go a long way in ensuring that the first impression he makes on a citizen during a call is a positive one. Are your boots shined? Is your uniform clean and pressed? Are you properly groomed? Too often, we let these crucial aspects of our appearance go by the wayside, all the while not realizing the impact it's having on how both our peers and the public view us.

"But this issue goes well-beyond the uniform. It's up to us individually to learn how to properly take care of ourselves. I've never thought health and wellness were elevated to the level they needed to be in order for people to take them seriously. Proper nutrition, getting enough sleep, staying physically fit, and ensuring your proficiency level as a police officer continues to improve are all important aspects of being professional. Sure, the agency's culture can certainly have a profound effect on professionalism, but at the end of the day, it is our individual responsibility and must come from within."

It was obvious what Jason liked the most about his career, so I asked him what was the most difficult for him.

His response was different from many. "The easy way out of explaining the most difficult part of a police career is to follow the standard societal norm of presenting our individual 'highlight reels' of incidents and cases, focusing on the positive things, and simply ignoring the bad. But that isn't a true reflection of us, and I am certainly no different.

"As motivated and ambitious as I was during my career, there was never a proper focus on what was going on at home. I know that now, but that is only after being divorced twice and doing my best to evolve as a person. Balancing work and life is incredibly difficult. Since most of us start our police career at a very young age, there's a lack of the skills and life experience necessary to cope with the demands of the job while maintaining stability in our personal lives.

"Right away, we're faced with the pressure to succeed. The paramilitary aspect of a police department means you are immediately thrust into an ultracompetitive work environment. It's a place where the ability to get promoted or work a new assignment depends on a combination of your relationships, work ethics, skills, and determination to be better than your peers. Some choose to do the minimum, but others like myself would set goals that I would put a maximum effort into achieving. But that can come at a cost at home. We all know that."

As Jason has talked about, learning to balance the job and home life can be challenging. I asked what he personally did on his off-duty time to destress or rejuvenate. Everyone has their own path, and as you might suspect by now, Jason's involved fitness.

"Staying active and physically fit was always my top priority. The bonus for me was that I have always enjoyed it. In 1998, as a member of the academy staff, I was sent to the Law Enforcement Fitness Trainer course at the Cooper Institute in Dallas, Texas. To say that class and certification had a huge impact on me would be an understatement.

"I was already training in mixed martial arts typically two to three days a week and was also a life-long basketball player. I played in regular leagues and Police Olympics tournaments, but the Cooper Institute opened my eyes to the aspects of being fit that I had been missing. Better nutrition, strength and conditioning, proper sleep, and the increased desire to be in the best shape possible began to consume me and still does to this day.

"The next year, I attended the Master Fitness Trainer Course at the Cooper Institute and further accelerated my knowledge in the areas of weight training, cardiovascular training, and nutrition. Today, some twenty-three years later, the principles I have learned and put into my daily routine are what drive me.

"As a retiree, I prioritize working out five days per week while eating a health-conscience diet consisting of foods that will fuel my training and ensure optimal performance. That's how I think now, and that's how I thought during my career, though getting a large number of my peers to agree with me was another issue entirely."

Every first responder has what I call a career-defining moment. Some are similar in nature; some have surprised me. Sadly, for too many, this moment involves the loss of a coworker. Jason was no different.

He shared, "There were a number of funerals I attended early in my career for officers who had died by suicide, in car accidents, or from other causes. They're all tough, but the one that really became difficult to process was that of Sergeant Henry Prendes. On February 1, 2006, he was ambushed on a domestic violence call and shot by a suspect at close range with an assault rifle. At the time, this was our agency's first police officer shot and killed in eighteen years, which predated my time in the department by three years.

"I'm not sure if this would qualify as a career-defining moment, but I was presiding over academy class 1/2006 as the academy sergeant on the day Henry was shot. That meant I had to inform the class what had happened, which was difficult given the circumstances. We were all in shock, and now I had the responsibility of supporting the class and ensuring that they continued to stay focused on their training, despite the tragedy that had just occurred.

"Henry and I had played basketball together, and we had worked together as fellow field training officers at the Southeast Area Command from 1996–1997. Though I remember standing in front of the class and telling them about what had happened to Henry, I don't recall exactly what I said. It's a blur. Several of our recruits decided law enforcement wasn't for them that day, citing the shooting as a dose of reality they weren't ready to deal with.

"Sadly, Henry was the first of many who have been shot and killed in the line of duty over the last fifteen-plus years with LVMPD. None of them were any easier to cope with."

At the very beginning of Jason's story, I mentioned that Jason and I had met through social media. While scrolling through one particular site, I came across Jason and was surprised to see that he had made some documentaries After checking out his website, I rented one of his films, *Repeat Offender*, and watched it. I was so impressed with it that I rented another one and then another.

Some law enforcement officers struggle with what they want to do once they retire. Jason wasn't one of those, and he created Lightning Digital Entertainment. This is a very different path but one that merges two of his passions and talents, law enforcement and filmmaking. While not the only reason I wanted Jason in the book, this seamless blending was a major factor.

Of course, I had to start at the beginning and asked him why filmmaking and how did he get his start.

He responded, "I have always been a big fan of movies and had an interest in how they were made since I was a young child.

"Starting in the late 1970s, I used to read a couple of now out-of-print magazines called *Cinefex* and *Starlog*, both of which covered the technical side of filmmaking and special effects. The idea of having the skills to tell a story by way of a film intrigued me. Of course, doing so would've been out of the question prior to the digital age, given the costs associated with film, equipment, and the necessary crew, which was reserved primarily for people who were lucky enough to make a movie within the studio system.

"The idea of becoming an independent filmmaker really began to take shape while working at the academy. The department's video unit, made up at the time of Don Bell and Shelley Vorce, was stationed in our building. After seeing them work on a variety of training videos for our staff, I began to pick their brain.

"In the late 1990's, rather than utilizing film or giant news-style beta cams costing over $100,000 at the time, Don and Shelley introduced me to the world of mini dv tapes, which were then digitized on a linear computer-based editing system much like we still use today. And the best part? These new tools were affordable for everyone which meant it would no longer require millions of dollars to produce my own films. I guess you could say that was the moment this indie filmmaker was officially born.

"I spent a lot of my time off as an assistant to both Don and Shelley. They were gracious enough to teach me their craft. It wasn't long before my abilities began to reach a level where I knew my way around a camera, lighting a scene, and editing raw video into a final product."

Jason spent the next several years learning the various technical skills required. He started Lightning Digital Entertainment and began filming commercials, events, and training videos under the banner of his production company. He made his first $250 production fee in 2003 for producing a commercial for a gadget that, when installed, would allow someone who owned a vehicle with pop-up headlights to utilize them as a "personal flirtation device" by winking at someone. The device was called "The Winker!"

Having watched several of his films, I asked him why his primary focus had become documentaries.

He explained, "There are several reasons. The first is this idea that has bothered me for quite some time where the journalists we see in mainstream media are anointed as experts in every topic that comes along and polarizes our country.

"We've seen this with the pandemic, and we have certainly witnessed this false expertise when it comes to issues involving police officers. Quite frankly, I believe these are OUR stories to tell and are not being conveyed accurately. They're filtered through the politics of any given network and then read by a talking head who is offering a biased opinion rather than reporting the news.

"When it comes to those critical issues that police officers deal with each day, I feel the true message is lost amongst the noise of special interests and political agendas. Thus, my desire became to focus solely on making feature documentary films that are not only pro-police, but actually tell the stories from the perspective of someone who has truly walked in those shoes and understands the issues.

"I am driven by an enormous responsibility I've created for myself by becoming a filmmaker who focuses on telling true stories within the documentary space. I don't have a team, nor are my projects funded in advance. In order to produce a feature film, I need to possess the ability to take the project from pre-production (concept, writing, casting, location scouting) through production (principal photography) and ending with postproduction (editing, color grading, sound mixing). Even then, the job isn't complete because now you have to figure out how to market and distribute the film. It's a process that can take as much as a year or more, but the end result is always something I am proud of. I will never stop placing an emphasis on telling the stories that mainstream media ignores.

"With making films, there is also a fear of failure. Entering into the highly competitive world of filmmaking wasn't easy, nor did I expect it to be. There is no shortage of people who have the same skill set as I do, with their own stories to tell and topics they are passionate about. No one is your friend in this business. In some ways, I've found my overall impression of the film world to be even more cutthroat than police work. And that's saying something."

The first film of Jason's that I watched was titled *Repeat Offender*. It was Jason's second film and based on the book by the same title. Having worked in investigations for fifteen years, I found the film captivating and believe that any detective working in the property crimes or burglary arena should see the film.

I asked Jason why this film.

He responded, "After my first film, *The Basketball Family*, came out, I was looking for my next project. I had recently read Detective Bradley Nickell's 2015 true crime book *Repeat Offender*, which chronicled his nearly ten-year investigation of one of

Las Vegas's most notorious career criminals. Brad also worked for LVMPD, and I knew him. So I decided to call and see if he would be interested in allowing me to adapt his book into a feature documentary.

"It was released in 2019, and I refer to it as a detective masterclass. As all of us know in law enforcement, property crimes are frequently pled out to lesser charges and are often not a priority for the District Attorney's Office. The tenacity Brad showed during this investigation led to a multi-million-dollar stolen property recovery and triggered a murder-for-hire plot against Brad, the district attorney, and the judge in the case.

"It is truly a remarkable story. My main focus was always to articulate how Brad caught the suspect rather than highlighting the suspect himself. Brad's detective work is the only reason one of the most prolific career criminals in our city's history is serving six consecutive life terms behind bars. A lesser effort means the crook would still be terrorizing his victims today."

I watched two more of Jason's films—*The Wounded Blue* and *Voices of the Blue*. In my opinion, these films should be watched by everyone working in the law enforcement profession. Police officers are not treated or supported the same by all law enforcement agencies within our great country. Some are left to fend for themselves after life-altering and critical incidents and injuries.

Jason's films should also be seen by people outside the law enforcement profession whether they're supporters or not. I spent twenty-six years in the profession, and some aspects of these films were still sad and eye-opening.

I asked Jason why he chose to do these two films.

He said, "I had a friend named Randy Sutton who had had a stroke while on-duty in his patrol car. As a result, he retired from

LVMPD in 2011. Afterward, he became involved with helping injured and disabled police officers.

"Randy knew I had recently released my first film *The Basketball Family*, and he had also served as the narrator for my second film *Repeat Offender*, which I was putting the finishing touches on when he called wanting to meet for lunch.

"During our meeting, he explained that he wanted to create a charitable organization to help further his efforts to assist injured officers. We also discussed his desire to produce a documentary film with stories that had influenced him to form his organization.

"With Randy as an executive producer, we released *The Wounded Blue: Service. Sacrifice. Betrayed* in 2019 and gained critical acclaim, particularly within the law enforcement community. People finally saw the truth being told on the issues of post-traumatic stress disorder (PTSD), suicide, and the financial hardships an officer can incur after being injured during a critical incident.

"My film *Voices of the Blue* is a six-part docuseries that serves as a sequel to *The Wounded Blue*. It continues telling the stories of injured and disabled law enforcement officers throughout the country. People generally believe that when an officer is involved in a shooting and is injured as a result, the department will take care of them both medically and financially. This is simply not true.

"In fact, with the majority of police departments having less than fifty officers, most agencies are not prepared for the day when one of their own is involved in a critical incident, nor do they have programs in place to ensure they are taken care of in the aftermath. In reality, many departments push the injured officer to come back to work, even when they may not be ready physically or emotionally. Often, when the officer is not able to return to work within one year, some agencies will fire that officer. The way we treat our cops is truly disgusting."

Jason's most recent film was a documentary about a cheer squad. I couldn't help but ask why he created something so different.

He said, "My first film, *The Basketball Family*, was a sports documentary about retired NBA player Doug Lee who became the head coach of a local high school team. I knew if the opportunity presented itself, I would certainly be thrilled to do another sports film.

"In 2017, a local cheer gym called ASMT Cheer Academy contacted me to create a video about their classes, teams, and instructors. Of course, this was made possible by my significant other, LaDawn Grant. At the time, she was the head coach for the Becker Middle School Competitive Cheer Team.

"As you would imagine, I was immersed in the sport of competitive cheer as a result and instantly admired the skills each of these athletes possessed as well as the months of grueling practices they endured prior to their season.

"In 2019, LaDawn announced that after twenty-three years of coaching cheer, she was stepping down at the conclusion of the 2020 season. That's where the light went on in my head. I had been shooting *Voices of the Blue* but was looking for another project to shoot in the first quarter of 2020. Perfect, right?

"I followed the team from their first practice all the way through the unceremonious end to their season as a result of the pandemic. This film, titled *The Making of a Cheer Team*, premiered at the 2021 Silver State Film Festival and was released simultaneously on multiple platforms."

Jason's latest film was released in September of 2022. He explained, "This documentary is called *Wrist Lock* and chronicles the martial arts influence on police use of force. Every technique we teach police officers in the area of defensive tactics is derived from the martial arts.

"The film argues that if we know martial artists have reached a high level of proficiency through regular training and practice over a period of decades, then why do we attempt to teach police officers the same techniques but don't require them to practice regularly once they graduate from the academy? Many states and agencies don't require recertification in defensive tactics after the academy. As a result, these skills diminish over time and not be available to an officer when needed the most.

"The film follows Master Martial Artist and Retired Police Sergeant Jon Gentile on a journey to discover the effect that a lack of training in this area has had on law enforcement. It looks at how agencies are sending officers into encounters that may require a use of force without the proficiency necessary to be successful. Featured are segments with retired police trainers who are also high-level martial artists in disciplines such as Brazilian Jiu-Jitsu, Muay Thai, karate, judo, and more, as well as experts in the police training, medical, and coaching realms.

"In addition, we examine the epidemic of obesity in law enforcement and the health consequences that come from being unfit over a long career. If officers are not physically fit, how can they be expected to be successful when they put their hands on someone in a use-of-force situation? Further explored is the topic of mental health and how common it may be for an officer who is mentally compromised to either underact or overact in a use-of-force scenario.

"I think we can all agree that these are three major components to any situation that requires force. An officer must be proficient in defensive tactics while also being physically and mentally fit. This leads to a discussion on the idea that agencies should create programs where our officers are trained more like professional athletes. It is crucial we address these issues head-on as a profession, particularly given the climate law enforcement faces today. We need to be better."

I had the opportunity to preview *Wrist Lock*. It's an excellent film that captures everything Jason talked about. It would be extremely beneficial for citizen groups who truly want a better understanding of the use of force by the police, law enforcement administrators, and all law enforcement officers.

When people choose a name for their business, there is often a reason or meaning behind it. The name that Jason gave to his company Lighting Digital Entertainment was a combination of two things.

He explained, "It's a homage to James Cameron, the director I admire the most and the advent of the digital filmmaking age that has given myself and so many others the tools, ability, and opportunity to create the films that tell the stories that are important to us."

Jason's films have received several awards.

- Platinum Reel Award - *The Basketball Family* - 2016 Nevada International Film Festival

- Bronze Award - *The Basketball Family* - 2017 Spotlight Documentary Awards

- Award of Recognition - *The Basketball Family* - 2017 Impact Doc Awards

- Best Documentary Feature (Nominee) - *The Basketball Family* - 2017 Top Indie Film Awards

- Best Editing (Nominee) - *The Basketball Family* - 2017 Top Indie Film Awards
- Silver Screen Award - *Repeat Offender* - 2018 Nevada International Film Festival
- Bronze Award - *Repeat Offender* - 2019 Spotlight Documentary Awards
- Award of Merit - *Repeat Offender"* - 2019 Impact Doc Awards
- Bronze Telly Award - *The Wounded Blue* - 2019 Telly Awards
- Bronze Award - *The Wounded Blue-* 2019 Spotlight Documentary Awards
- Award of Merit - *The Wounded Blue* - 2019 Impact Doc Awards
- Best Editing/Feature Film - *The Wounded Blue* - 2019 Silver State Film Festival
- Bronze Telly Award - *Voices of the Blue* - 2021 Telly Awards
- Official Selection - *The Making of a Cheer Team* - 2021 Silver State Film Festival
- Award of Recognition - *The Making of a Cheer Team* - 2022 Impact Doc Awards
- Bronze Award - *The Making of a Cheer Team* - 2022 Spotlight Documentary Awards

When Jason agreed to let me tell his story, I asked him what he hoped people garnered from reading this book and the previous two volumes.

He answered, "There's no questioning the value of reinforcing the idea that police officers are normal, everyday people who happen to find themselves doing extraordinary things at work. We all have the same problems and issues as everyone else. There certainly isn't a class in the police academy that will help you stay married or financially healthy, nor do police officers avoid the regular unforeseen pitfalls of life.

"But on top of the standard family and professional issues, officers must also deal with high levels of stress that can come in the form of critical incidents, horrific crime scenes, violent encounters with suspects, and internal politics. I know your prior volumes of *Behind and Beyond the Badge* have effectively brought forth the stories which humanize our profession."

Jason shared these final thoughts: "If you are a current law enforcement officer or considering the profession, it is up to you to ensure you remain proficient in the skills required for your job. It is up to you to stay physically fit and healthy. It is up to you to take care of your mental health.

"Unfortunately, most agencies will not require any of this from you. There is a culture within the law enforcement profession that we are all familiar with. It encourages a number of detrimental habits to your overall health and well-being. Engaging less in activities such as drinking alcohol, smoking, and eating a poor diet, while instead drinking more water, eating nutritious food, and working out regularly will have a profound and noticeable impact on your performance at work and long-term ability to stay healthy when you reach retirement."

Jason, thank you for your service to your country and community.

Jason can be reached at:

Website: LightningDigitalEntertainment.com

Twitter: @JasonHarney72 or @LDE_Films and he is also on LinkedIn: https://www.linkedin.com/in/jason-har-ney-720bb7122/

EIGHT

Lieutenant Maria Mercurio

Tallahassee Police Department (Florida): 22 Years
Florida State University Police Department: 2 years
Active Duty: 24 Years of Service

I met Maria when she began her career at the Tallahassee Police Department (TPD) in 1999. At that time, I was the sergeant supervising our department's Homicide Unit, and our interactions were limited to brief encounters at crime scenes.

When I was hired at TPD in 1979, I was one of only five women who were sworn police officers. That number continued to grow throughout my career. When I retired in 2006, I continued to follow Maria's career and many of the other amazing female officers.

In 2021, Maria and I were part of a team that played in our local Police Unity Tour Golf Tournament. Our other two team members were some of the first recruits to come through my patrol squad when I was a field training sergeant. They also are retired. We had a blast that day, and it wasn't only about the golf but the fun day together. Maria also started participating in another charity that is near and dear to me—the Mahatma Shuffle.

The more I got to know Maria, I was convinced she would be a great story to tell for *Behind and Beyond the Badge – Volume III*. She is dedicated, loves her profession, and gives so much more than is required.

When I began my career, I was the only female officer on my shift for over a year. I had no other female officers to look up to or seek guidance from. At times, it was stressful and truly a "wing-it" mentality.

Maria always has a smile on her face and is absolutely the happiest and most positive law enforcement officer I know. Without a doubt, she does the job for all of the right reasons and is someone that others should strive to emulate, especially female officers. She has become the mentor I didn't have.

She shared, "As far as I can remember, I wanted to be a police officer. As a kid, my favorite toy was a Lone Ranger set that included a gun belt, white cowboy hat, and a star badge. The idea of catching bad guys and having nonstop adventures won me over. As I grew up, my childhood dream job never faded, mostly due to television shows like *CHiPs*, *Miami Vice*, and *Cagney and Lacey*.

"Sounds silly, but I was intrigued by the uniform, patrol car, police gadgets, and the ability to save the day. These reasons developed into more meaningful ones while attending college and completing an internship with the Leon County Sheriff's Office. I rode along with deputies and responded to multiple calls and crime scenes over the course of several months.

"I recall seeing my first dead body, which happened to be severely decomposed. The smell lingered with me for days. That didn't deter me, and I was eager to see and learn more. I witnessed deputies intervene in domestic situations and a myriad of other calls for service which solidified my desire to become a police officer. I saw with my own eyes the real-life impacts an officer can have on a person or situation, and I was sold. No two days were the same. The wide variety of job duties that were available made me want to continue my career path toward this honorable profession."

Maria graduated from Florida State University (FSU) in 1996 with a bachelor of science degree in criminology and criminal justice. After graduation, she entered the Pat Thomas Law Enforcement Academy, attending classes fulltime during the day and working as a server and bartender at night and on the weekends. It took months of hard work, but Maria graduated from the academy in August 1997 and began her search for a law enforcement job.

Four months later in January 1998, Maria was hired by the FSU Police Department. She expounded on the beginning of her career. "I worked uniform patrol and quickly became IPMBA (International Police Mountain Bike Association) certified so I could patrol campus on a bike. As a young, eager cop, I hit the ground running, making narcotic arrests and underage-drinking cases. It was here where I first got involved with the Rape Aggression Defense (R.A.D.) women's self-defense program.

"Although I enjoyed working with a great group of officers at FSUPD, I found campus police work to be limiting, and I wanted to expand my career opportunities. I applied with TPD. After two years of service with FSUPD, I was hired with the Tallahassee Police Department in December 1999."

As Maria had mentioned, she felt a law enforcement career would offer many opportunities to serve her community in different capacities. During her twenty-two years with TPD, she has worked as a patrol officer, field training officer, and investigator, and she has worked in several other units as an officer, sergeant, and lieutenant. She is currently the supervisor of the Internal/External Affairs Bureau, which includes the Training Unit, Special Events Unit, and the Community Relations Unit.

With the different areas that she's worked, I asked Maria what her favorite assignment was. She told me that she has enjoyed each position tremendously over the years, but one of her favorites was Special Investigations, more commonly known as Vice and Narcotics.

She elaborated. "Some of my most memorable experiences have been working undercover operations posing as a prostitute or drug user so that I could purchase illegal drugs. Unlike the movie *Pretty Woman*, I would dress in a tattered tank top and stain covered shorts. I would douse my hair with gel to make it look unkept followed by digging my nails in the dirt to not look so clean.

"I never realized my acting skills would be put to the test as I had street-side encounters with the johns negotiating a price for an array of sex acts. I had men grab my breasts, say not-so-nice things to me, and ejaculate as I stood at their car door window, all while having a hot, uncomfortable body wire concealed in my bra to capture recorded audio from each encounter.

"I juggled so many variables of the operation while keeping myself focused on remaining in my undercover role and, most importantly, keeping myself safe. I knew and trusted my squad mates who always had my back. Working so closely with fellow officers builds teamwork and trust that's important so you can stay focused on going home at the end of each shift.

"The assignment that has my heart, though, is Crime Prevention/Community Relations. I have responded to countless calls relating to robberies, shootings, stabbings, sexual assaults, and many more during my career. Each call had a victim, and I have always wanted to do something more than just take a report and be reactive. Educating citizens on prevention strategies and personal safety became a passion of mine. It was in this assignment that I started the R.A.D. (Rape Aggression Defense) women's self-defense program at TPD."

R.A.D. is a system of physical self-defense techniques and risk avoidance for women. The program includes educational components comprised of lecture, discussion, and physical resistive strategies. R.A.D. teaches students to defend themselves and to recognize dangerous situations.

As I mentioned earlier, Maria first became involved with R.A.D. while working at FSUPD. She further explained, "I recognized the positive impact it had on women and saw firsthand how empowered they were at the completion of the course. After working dozens of cases where females were victims of various crimes, I wanted to make R.A.D. available for all women, not just college students. While working in the Community Relations Unit, I proposed starting this program at TPD and obtained grants and funding to get it up and running.

"R.A.D. began at TPD in 2006, and we have been teaching it ever since. Then I went on to complete the advanced training course for it in 2007. R.A.D. is taught by female TPD officers and assisted by male TPD officers in the scenario portion of the program. I coordinate all the classes, sign up all the students, schedule all the instructors, facilitate the training venue, advertise the classes, and serve as the lead instructor. We teach six to seven classes each year and have taught over 1,300 women through the years.

"The program teaches risk awareness, risk reduction, risk recognition, and risk avoidance. We want women to avoid hazardous situations by recognizing potential dangers. The goal is to prevent an attack rather than fear it. We impart confidence building through stances, verbal direction, and basic self-defense techniques like punches, kicks, blocks, and many others. Education may be the only thing that can turn instinctive fear into knowledge, power, and personal abilities.

"This program is my passion project. I have sacrificed many Saturdays and days off teaching because I believe in it. I know we are making a difference in women's lives because I've seen it. We've had dozens of survivors of domestic abuse, sexual abuse, and various other victims of crimes or circumstances go through this program. They have broken down in tears and fought through demons. It has helped heal them from the past. Those who have never experienced victimization but feared it are now empowered and have a plan.

"The women who attend R.A.D. are everyday women ranging in age from twelve years old to seniors. I've taught three generations of women from one family—a grandmother, daughter, and granddaughter.

"We also teach a radKIDS class, which is a **Children's Safety Education program taught by certified TPD officers.** It empowers children and parents with a revolutionary skill-based curriculum that strengthens children's personal boundaries and parental confidence. The radKIDS curriculum replaces fear with knowledge, skill, and power by enhancing a child's critical thinking abilities and physical resistance skills. Our programs provide the opportunity for children to recognize, avoid, resist, and if necessary, escape violence or harm while remaining joyful and safer in our world today.

"I have received emails, calls, and visits from past students who have shared their prevention stories or new outlook on life as it related to personal safety. I am so proud of every student who has gone through the course. R.A.D women ROCK!"

Maria shared a couple of comments and reviews that she'd received from past students of the R.A.D. program. I thought that any one of those comments might be considered one of the nicest compliments that she'd ever received as an officer. But I was wrong.

She shared, "A few years ago, I was working an officer-friendly type of event and was interacting with an autistic child. The mother stood back and watched as I allowed him to put on a spare ballistic-vest I had in my patrol car and garnished him with a sticker police badge. After our encounter was over, she approached me and said, 'Thank you.' I thought she was referring to me interacting with her child, but she went on to tell me I had investigated a sexual battery she had survived over seventeen years earlier.

"The woman said she couldn't have done it without me, and my kindness made that horrible situation bearable. I immediately recalled her and her case. The suspect was found not guilty at trial. All these years, I have carried the burden that I let her down. Maybe if I had done something different in the investigation, the verdict would have been different. We embraced, and I believe we both healed a little bit more that day."

The encounter with this woman is what Maria finds to be the most rewarding part of her job. She said, "For me, it's being able to make a difference in someone's life. Having been a law enforcement officer in Tallahassee for twenty-four years, I can't go to the grocery store or somewhere in public without someone recognizing me and saying hello. Often, it's the women who have taken my R.A.D. class over the years, and at times, they greet me with a defensive stance learned from the class. Sometimes, it's a resident of a neighborhood who I assisted with their neighborhood watch group, or a child that I read a book to in school.

"I recently received a social media message and didn't recognize the name. I opened the message, and it was from a man who wanted to thank me for not arresting him twenty-three years ago for underage drinking. I recalled the kid because he lived in a dormitory that I patrolled often. After our first encounter, I kept tabs on him to stay out of trouble. He told me that I kept him from going down the wrong path, and after all these years, he wanted to thank me. He shared with me his career success and the beautiful family he had. I don't do my job to receive thanks or accolades, but it's the little things, knowing I've helped in some way, that feel good."

With all that Maria has done and been involved with, I asked her what the most difficult part of the job was for her. She said, "The hardest part is seeing true monsters that live among us who commit horrid acts against others. My time spent working in the Special Victims Unit were some of the most difficult times, working with survivors ranging from young children to seniors. One of my youngest victims was only six years old when she contracted gonorrhea from her mother's boyfriend who was molesting her. Seeing the innocence of a child be taken and knowing she will never get that back. . .those cases stick with you forever. We do the job to help those who can't help themselves."

Maria also participates with the TPD Habitat for Humanity team that helps the organization build homes in the Tallahassee community. When I asked her why, she answered, "I am so grateful for the life and opportunities I've had in my life; I need to give back. I have always had a roof over my head, a warm bed to sleep in, and food on my table.

"Over my career, I have seen many that have not. Habitat for Humanity allows me to help build a home for a family and give them the opportunity to feel proud of home ownership. Besides the feel-good side, another bonus is working alongside my fellow coworkers in a more laid-back atmosphere. We get to trade in the gun belts for construction belts. I get to recognize talents that I never knew some of them had, and I also get to see how bad some are at painting or hammering. Overall, just having fun doing something good for another."

For the past fourteen years, she has served on the executive board of the 501(c)3 nonprofit Lincoln Center Foundation. She explained, "The Foundation sponsors the Lincoln Center Boxing Club whose overall mission is to promote a positive self-image through the art of boxing.

"Youth, ages eight thought eighteen, develop learning techniques to control impulsiveness, anger, and alternative behavior responses by being provided a safe, structured boxing program that gives them a positive outlet for aggressive and hostile energy. The Foundation also partners with the Lincoln Neighborhood Service Center (a City of Tallahassee neighborhood center) to provide community programs such as a summer enrichment program, senior computer and exercise classes, educational workshops, and other activities that enhance the lives of community residents.

"Although I don't have children, kids hold a special place in my heart, especially those who have some disadvantages in life. I have been fortunate to grow up involved with sports, received an excellent education, and have a loving family. I feel a sense of obligation to make a difference in a kid's life."

For the past two years, Maria has been involved with the Big Brothers Big Sisters Bigs in Blue mentoring program, a nationwide initiative launched by Big Brothers Big Sisters (BBBS). The program connects youth with police officers in communities, building strong, trusting, and lasting relationships. These relationships can help children develop into confident adults and help build stronger bonds between law enforcement and the families they serve.

Maria added, "I became involved when the BBBS of America came to the police department looking for volunteer officers. Having mentored with the Leon County Schools in the past, I was immediately interested in this one-on-one program. Since I enjoy working with kids, I signed up. I was matched with a ten-year-old boy and have made such great memories with him over these past two and a half years.

"Having two sisters growing up, I have always wanted a little brother. BBBS made this a reality. My 'Little' (as the younger counterpart is often lovingly referred to within BBBS) and I have enjoyed outdoors activities like fishing, football, hiking, soccer, and his favorite, getting ice-cream. Although fun seems to be our priority, we squeeze in schoolwork and strive to be the best person we can. I have seen such growth and maturity with my 'Little' during our time we spend together. I am so proud of him and look forward to continuing our relationship.

"It has been so rewarding to work with a child and see the positive progress they have made in academics, social skills, and other areas, helping them reach their potential and not get lost. I am thankful to have gained lasting relationships and memories that make it all worth it."

Maria helps in other ways that also build those lasting memories that are important to her. Living in Florida, the potential for being in the path of a hurricane is a yearly reality that all first responder agencies prepare for. At some point, the community that you live in or one nearby will be directly impacted. When that happens, everyone and every agency comes together to help. Law enforcement agencies are often the first to send help.

When Hurricane Andrew made landfall in South Florida in 1992, I was deployed along with two other officers and our City of Tallahassee utility crew. We were the first of several teams who rotated deployment to help out. I grew up in Florida and had been through many hurricanes, but my three weeks in the Miami area was truly humbling. The amount of devastation and hardship was unimaginable.

Maria deployed for the relief efforts related to Hurricane Michael in October 2018. TPD was requested to assist in Jackson County due to the devastation the area suffered with downed trees, loss of electricity, and the destruction of homes and businesses. She supervised a squad of fellow volunteer officers assigned to work twelve-hour midnight shifts for four days.

Maria said, "We guarded various locations around the county to prevent thefts and keep the peace. Due to working mostly at night, I didn't have too many interactions with citizens. Prior to the deployment, I made goodie bags to give to those who may need a small treat to lift their spirits. While staying at a hotel during the deployment, I was able to gift these bags to some area families who had been displaced. It's the small things, such as seeing smiles on their faces and giving them a hug of comfort during difficult times…more reasons why I love what I do."

Every first responder has that one career-defining moment, some more than one. Maria shared hers.

"I have always tried to keep some separation in my personal life and my professional life," she started. "Most of my friends are non-law enforcement, and my hobbies and interest don't revolve around guns or police-related activities.

"A career-defining moment for me occurred when I was off-duty. I was visiting close friends out of town, and one friend did not show up for a planned outing. We called other friends and checked locations where she might have been but with no luck. My friend suffered from a medical condition that caused her physical and emotional pain, so the concern grew.

"I began working in 'cop mode,' running through options to find her, but as the hours went by, there was still no word from her. We contacted local law enforcement to file a missing person's report, and they assisted with the search. We located a recent credit card purchase of a firearm and ammunition. My fears grew worse. I knew I had to stay strong for my friends and do what I do best—manage a critical incident.

"I was the go-between for the patrol officers and my friends. My fears became reality when the officers called me over to their cars to tell me my friend had died by suicide.

My two worlds collided, and I had to deliver a death notification to my closest friends. I always hated to do death notifications because telling someone their loved one had died stays with you forever. Seeing such sadness and pain sucks. Sometimes, I feel like this job has made me the most emotionless emotional person on this planet."

I asked Maria what she felt was the most important quality for a law enforcement officer to have. She replied, "There are so many important qualities an officer must possess, but I think treating people with dignity and respect is top on my list. We interact with people going through incredible hardships, so we must show compassion while remaining professional.

"I am currently a member of the Tallahassee Police Department's Special Response Team (SRT) and serve a leadership role on the team. The team's role is to ensure public safety through crowd management, crowd dispersal, and the protection of life and property during incidents of civil unrest.

"In 2020, our city had experienced local protests resulting in the SRT team deploying several times. One took place outside the police station where hundreds of protesters were opposing the police. Hoping for the best but fearing the worst, we listened to the chanting of the large crowd and read the hateful handmade signs they held. After a time, the crowds dispersed without any incidents, and only a few protesters remained. Another member of the team and I went outside to assess the exterior gate area.

"We encountered a small group of young adult protesters who eagerly approached us. We engaged them in conversation, and although their signs referred to cops as 'Killer Pigs,' I felt the need to listen to what they had to say. As I listened, I may not have agreed with all their opinions but gave them the respect to speak.

"I provided my perspective on some of the scenarios we discussed and explained the fears an officer may have and reasons why we may react in certain ways to certain situations. We ended our lengthy conversation with handshakes and smiles. I believe we made a small dent in humanizing our profession that day."

Professionally, Maria stays busy and engaged, so I asked, "What do you like to do when you're off-duty?" Because I've seen her posts on social media, her answer came as no surprise.

She answered, "As each year goes by, I recognize the importance of having hobbies and interests outside the job. I love to travel and see the world. I also love to cook and eat. I combine these loves and have been fortunate enough to visit several continents. So many places, so little time.... or maybe money!

"When I'm not traveling and tasting delicious foods, I enjoy spending time with family and friends. I love to fish, camp, kayak, and just spend time outdoors. I am a Florida girl who loves her beach and sunshine. My travel companion in love and life is my wife Jennifer. She is my sidekick in all things fun. I also have two fur babies, Belle and Izzy, the sweetest little pups on this earth."

Throughout her career, Maria has received individual and unit awards:

- 2006 Crime Prevention Unit award
- 2009 Walter A. McNeil Distinguished Service Award Runner-up
- 2010 Meritorious Service Award
- 2011 Walter A. McNeil Distinguished Service Award Recipient
- 2013 Special Investigations Unit award

I asked Maria, "What do you hope people learn from reading the *Behind and Beyond the Badge* book series?"

She answered, "These books allow others to see how cops are just people doing the best they can in a tough profession. Those who don't work in this profession don't realize how much death and sadness we see. We respond to all deaths that don't occur in a hospital, which include homicides, natural deaths, suicides, traffic fatalities, and accidental deaths.

"Working in a city of over 250,000 people, we see these types of cases daily. We are called to do a job. Although we may feel an array of emotions, we must mask what we feel inside to get the case solved or closed. No one wants a cop to respond to a scene and break down in tears. That does come with a price. I can't drive around the city without passing certain locations and recalling where victims have taken their last breaths. You try to not think about them, but I have accepted that those memories will always be with me.

"I was a rookie cop when the deadly 9/11 attack on our country occurred. When the planes hit, I was asleep because I had worked the midnight shift the previous night. I was woken up by a phone call and told the news. I hope the world always remembers those brave first responders who ran into those towers because that's what we do in crisis—run toward danger, not away from it. Policing is not for everyone, but those who are wanting to enter the profession, know that it is as much about helping people as it is about enforcing laws."

Family is important to Maria, and she shared, "My wife Jennifer is my rock. She supports me in all I do and understands the crazy hours, the 3:00 a.m. phone calls, and the missed birthday and holidays. She encourages me to share my feelings and unwind when she recognizes I'm not my normal self. Being the spouse of a cop can be stressful. I know I have given her added grey hairs due to getting home late and not having had the time to text or call because I was on a critical scene. I am thankful and lucky to have such an amazing partner in love and life.

"I have to say something about my mom and dad. They have always supported my law enforcement career and have instilled in me my work ethic and positive outlook on life. They've provided me with love and support, and my sisters would say my parents spoiled me because I'm the youngest. A shout out to my dad for teaching me outlets like sports, grilling, and fishing and my mom for working double shifts and weekends to put her three girls through private school. My fierce five-foot one-inch Japanese mom with her take-charge, get-it-done personality molded me into the person I am today. I have been called the happiest cop who is always smiling. I attribute this to my mentors, family, and friends. Life is pretty darn good."

Maria, thank you for your service and all that you do for your community.

NINE

Deputy Chief Mike Hartley

Bloomington Police Department (Minnesota): 25 Years
Tallahassee Police Department (Florida): 7 Years
Retired: 32 Years of Service

Mike and I have known each other for a long time, thirty-two years to be exact. I first met him when he was hired by the agency I was working at, the Tallahassee Police Department (TPD). While working there, he met a friend of mine, they fell in love, got married, and started a family. They are, in my opinion, the funniest couple I know! Eventually, they moved to Minnesota where Mike is from and where he continued his law enforcement career.

I've always liked Mike's story of how he chose the law enforcement profession, a profession that he loved and did for all the right reasons. Over the years, our relationship drifted a bit, but I kept watching his career move forward. Several months ago, the Bloomington Police Department (BPD) posted a video on their Facebook page about an initiative they had started, and Mike was explaining how it came to be.

I reached out to Mike, and we talked more about it. Not long after, I asked him if I could tell his story in *Behind and Beyond the Badge: Volume III.* He agreed.

Mike said, "In 1984, my dad asked me what I was going to do after high school. 'You're not tall enough to be a cop' wasn't the response I was looking for when I told him what I wanted to do. That night, in the basement of our Columbia Heights, Minnesota, home, he suggested I go into sales. My dad was partially right that evening; I was more wired for persuading and selling. But I believe that I wouldn't have reached the levels of success or effectiveness as an officer if I hadn't had the communication skills and personality to sell people into doing what I asked. Or, in some cases, ordered them to do.

"I was the first person in my family to go into police work. It was a combination of many influences that drove me in that direction. A high school teacher teaching a crime class, my early forays in the school patrol, and I would be remiss if I did not credit Cheap Trick's 'Dream Police' album. But what drew me in and kept me engaged in a thirty-two-year career, was the people I worked with and served. I like people. All people.

"In 1984, I started taking law enforcement classes at a local community college. I was young, and it was hard to focus. More than once I wondered if this was the right career path. Back then, police jobs were extremely competitive and scarce. My instructor for 'Introduction to Law Enforcement' looked out at the 200 students filling up the auditorium and stated that only one in twenty of us would actually work in the profession."

Mike continued taking classes. In 1987, as he neared the completion of his two-year degree in law enforcement, he ran into an old high school classmate. She told Mike that she had just been hired as a stenographer for the local branch of the FBI. They were hiring for many different non-agent positions.

Mike said, "On a wing and a prayer, I applied. In December of that year, I started working for them as a support employee, making $5.00 an hour.

"That job introduced me to working for an agency built on honor and respectability that held its employees to high standards. As a support employee, I did a myriad of things, including dispatching, managing case funds, and securing teletype correspondence. I continued my college education in hopes of applying for an agent position once I had obtained my four-year degree.

"In the meantime, I started working with a new agent who used to work at the Tallahassee Police Department (TPD). After talking with him, he convinced me to apply to TPD.

"During the interview process with TPD, I had to explain a trespass citation that I had received in 1984. I had gotten the citation while waiting in line overnight for Prince concert tickets. I guess that my employment with the FBI at that time helped soothe their concerns about a guy from Minnesota who had longer hair and listened to Prince. In 1990, I was hired by TPD, moved to Tallahassee, Florida, and began the police academy."

When Mike graduated from the academy, he was assigned to a field training squad. After completing that training, he began working as a solo status officer (one officer unit).

Mike said, "It was quite the adventure and cultural shock coming from Minnesota. I struggled early on to understand the accents (Southern) of certain dispatchers but slowly started to fit in. It was a young patrol division back then, and I worked with some really great squads.

"For six years, I primarily worked the south side of Talla-hassee, which had a higher concentration of African American residents. Back then, we wore 'serving since' pins under our name tags, and the criminal elements on the streets were not shy about reminding you that your lack of time in the department meant you carried no credibility with them. Crack cocaine was everywhere, and we would set up details that bull rushed deal-ers after surveillance observed narcotics transactions. At times, these fast-paced busts would end up in physical altercations, foot pursuits, and on occasion, a recovered gun.

"It was the endless cycle of street crimes being committed by the same people or someone new taking their place when an arrest and prosecution were made. Two Division 1 colleges were within walking distance of that neighborhood but may have well been in another country as far as they knew. It engrained in me the differences in opportunity that we all have.

"For instance, I used to work an off-duty security job in a Southside housing project. While making my rounds, all the lit-tle kids would run up and want to talk to me. I recall telling two brothers that I was going to soon fly home and visit my family in Minnesota. Their response was that they would never be able to fly on an airplane because their mother had never flown. And it also seemed that once the kids reached the age of twelve, they no longer wanted anything to do with the police and stopped talking with me.

"One year, my sister was visiting from Minnesota and went on a ride-along with me. We responded to a domestic call be-tween two female young adults. I approached the front door with my sister in tow. I could hear the physical altercation inside, and

I yelled, 'Police' as I swung open the door. A young child inside ran toward us, bypassing me and wrapping her arms around my sister's legs in a securing hug. My sister immediately started crying, and that image has stayed with me throughout my career.

"In 1996, I transferred to the Criminal Investigations Bureau (CIB) and worked on the Financial Crimes Squad. I worked for a great sergeant and really enjoyed investigating those complex fraud and forgery cases. I also graduated from Florida State University with my bachelor of arts degree in social science."

Mike's first child, his son, was also born that year. He and his wife Mary began talking about their future both professionally and where they wanted to raise their family.

Mike said, "I was able to convince Mary that raising a family up North was better than the hot South! I love Florida but really missed the seasonal changes and all of the outdoor activities that I grew up doing. In 1997, I accepted an officer position with the Bloomington Police Department (BPD). We made the move up North, trading hurricanes for snowstorms."

The BPD is a department with 123 sworn positions and thirty-seven non-sworn employees. It also has an internal jail with fifteen cells, but it's not a long-term holding facility. It's a temporary option before being transported to the Hannepin County Jail.

During his twenty-five years with BPD, Mike was a field training officer, a member of the SWAT team, a detective, a patrol sergeant, the department's training sergeant, a commander, the deputy chief, and served as the interim chief of police for fourteen months.

Work hours for police officers are often anything but normal. As a patrol officer, Mike told me that he was never a fan of working nights even though it's a big part of a police officer's life. In

Tallahassee, he worked the mid-shift that ended at 3:00 a.m. In Bloomington, he worked a power shift that ended at 2:00 a.m.

He added, "When I got promoted to sergeant, I went back to the night shift, and it was tough sleeping during the day with two little kids running around the house. I was on-call most of my career and had many SWAT callouts in the middle of the night. Once I was in the command staff, the calls came at any time regardless of the hour. As the deputy chief, I was the Public Information Officer (PIO). After several months, I convinced the media that it better be a significant call to warrant waking me up at 3:00 a.m."

I asked Mike about his time on the SWAT team. In addition to their normal duties for BPD, they also deployed to other areas in the country to assist with disasters. Mike mentioned two specific occasions.

"In 2005, the SWAT team was deployed to New Orleans following Hurricane Katrina. We were there for twenty days, providing relief to the New Orleans Police Department SWAT Team. The city was barely populated, and we stayed in campers that were donated by an RV dealership in Minnesota. Just the caravan down was an adventure and interesting, to say the least. We also assisted when the Interstate 35 West bridge collapsed into the Mississippi River. That massive bridge was heavily traveled and left one with an eerie feeling knowing that there were people and cars resting on the bottom of the river."

In 2013, Mike was named the Bloomington Police Department Officer of the Year. At that time, he was the sergeant supervising the Training Unit and had worked on expanding the department's training capabilities and formats.

He said, "I basically created more lifelike training scenarios and focused on high-probability encounter tactics. I supervised a great group of trainers who were just as motivated to move on from the stale old way of training police officers. We started incorporating physical and mental stress into our training and training scenarios."

Mike said that it doesn't hurt to have a good sense of humor to do the job but believes that the most important quality that a law enforcement officer needs to have is the ability to effectively communicate, both in speaking and with listening. Over the course of his career, he had many opportunities to do just that.

In 2014, Mike was the incident commander during the first Black Lives Matter (BLM) protest at the Mall of America. Approximately 3,000 protestors gathered inside the mall. This pre-planned event remained peaceful with a small number of arrests and no injuries to participants or law enforcement.

BPD also assisted the Minneapolis Police Department during the civil unrest following the killing of George Floyd. Mike said, "I was assigned to the Multi-Agency Command Center (MACC) for a few of those nights when the rioting and looting were at the worst. It was a chaotic experience. As an agency, we also supplied officers to the demonstrations following Daunte Wright's death in Brooklyn Center, Minnesota. There were members of our community who didn't think we should have provided assistance to these other surrounding communities, and communications played a big role in that.

"As the Interim Chief of Police, the most difficult part of that position for me was trying to balance the political with the practical. I knew the effects of decisions that were made over my head on the officers doing the job every day. Immediately following the death of George Floyd, the initial reaction of my city leaders was to ban all neck restraints. BPD had been training and utilizing the Lateral Vascular Neck Restraint for decades, and not one injury had occurred to anyone who had that technique applied to them.

"Before I could even have a discussion explaining the differences between the tactics utilized on George Floyd and the technique BPD utilized, people were also wanting to ban that option completely. That led to additional thoughts of banning crowd control tactics, including the chemical agents used to control riots. I will give our elected officials credit for listening and not rushing to ban what are important options when controlling a hostile crowd. Communications!"

Earlier, I mentioned a video I watched that had been posted on the BPD Facebook page. The video talks about an initiative named "Shift" that Mike had started at BPD. As I learned more about Shift, I could see how this video was the perfect example of what can happen when we speak and listen.

Mike said, "In June 2020, shortly after the death of George Floyd, members of our police department responded to a barricaded subject who threatened to shoot our officers if they entered his hotel room. During the previous week, this same individual had already confronted our officers in a highly agitated and belligerent manner while in possession of a handgun.

"As the hotel incident evolved into a barricaded subject and eventual SWAT activation, the subject began calling family and friends, telling them he was about to be shot and killed by the Bloomington Police Department. When I arrived that afternoon, I was met by the subject's mother. She demanded to go up to the room and talk to her son, though she wasn't allowed to in the middle of such a chaotic, dangerous situation. Also on scene was the subject's son as well as a handful of friends who responded after being called.

"One of the responding women was named Brenda Johnson. She had attended seminary school with the subject and approached me during the initial SWAT response. Amongst the early chaos caused by the subject's family and managing the SWAT response, this woman simply stated, 'I am here as a resource and to help anyway I can to prevent another black man from being killed.'

"The subject eventually surrendered. I will never forget the gratitude from his friends and family toward our officers on scene. In the weeks following the death of one African American man in Minneapolis at the hands of police, our department had worked through a confrontation to a peaceful resolution with another African American man, not unlike what we do just about every week as Bloomington police officers.

"Brenda Johnson grew up in North Minneapolis and worked at the Juvenile Detention Center (JDC) as an educational liaison. She is the single mother of two successful young adults and approaches life with an honest 'sometimes the truth hurts' attitude. She has worked through the years on various anti-violence campaigns in Minneapolis as she has watched the never-ending circle of violence unfold in her city including, on occasion, at the hands of police.

"Following the above incident, I texted Brenda and thanked her for being a resource that day instead of a liability. We decided to meet, and after an hour, it was clear that even amongst our differences, we agreed on so many other things like respect, parenting, and the great sounds of 80's music. At a time, when our country was and is so divided amongst racial and political lines, we began what has now become a friendship on what we have in common without dwelling on what we don't.

"It was during that first meeting that we talked about the historical divide between the police and African Americans. We talked about one another's perspectives and the value in learning how to look at something differently based on knowledge and experiences instead of historical falsehoods and misunderstandings. We decided to work together on a program that would bring officers and black community members together for tough but productive conversations about current relations and offer insight on what it is like to walk a day in one another's shoes. Success would not be based on proving who was right or wrong but rather a shift in the way we understand each other."

Mike sent an email to his department explaining what he had just told me and asked for eight sworn members who would find value in explaining the law enforcement profession but would also be willing to learn about the perspectives of members of their diverse community. The Shift would include an eight-hour training day followed by four two-hour meetings with community members that would take place in the evenings. These meetings would be facilitated by Brenda Johnson and Deb DeMeester, a former professor at St. Thomas University. Mike made it clear that it would not be a one-sided experience and explained specific objectives and goals.

He told me that it was an eye-opening, positive experience for everyone involved and well worth the effort. "When people are willing to speak honestly and listen with an open mind and heart, positive changes can happen."

Community is important to Mike, and he has served on a couple of charitable boards in Bloomington. He said, "Currently, I am President of the Bloomington Crime Prevention Association. This nonprofit holds a used book sale every year that generates funds for annual grants for crime prevention types of initiatives in the community. Schools, churches, youth groups, and victim advocacy groups are just some of the organizations that have received funding for crime prevention measures. The Book'Em Used Book Sale has made $170,000 annually over the last several years. I also served on the Beyond the Yellow Ribbon board, a military assistance organization that works with veterans and their families for a wide range of assistance initiatives."

Family is a priority for Mike. "Family is so important for that support structure throughout your career. My wife Mary had to manage our family through so many things that come with the job—late night callouts, command staff pages, media calls, to name a few. But my two kids also had to sacrifice so I could sleep when they were wide awake. They had to sit in classrooms as a curriculum was taught that painted their dad as a racist, knowing full-well that he wasn't. But I know in spite of all that, they were proud of the work I did. I always shared funny stories so that they could see the lighter side of the job as well. They knew and respected my police friends, who also didn't seem to fit the general negative narrative. I really can't put into words just how important Mary and my kids have been to me."

After serving as the interim police chief for fourteen months, I asked Mike why he didn't apply for the job permanently. He answered, "I never really planned a career path. Opportunities presented themselves, and I was fortunate to be selected. I didn't have much desire to be a chief. I'm a 'you get what you see, and you know what you get' kind of leader and loved being on the operational side of running a police department as a deputy chief.

"I'm not polished enough to play politics at the top position and didn't always tell the city manager what he wanted to hear. I wanted people who worked at BPD to like their jobs. I would tell all the new employees that my goal was to create a working environment where they arrived each day for work with a smile on their faces. Those smiles may disappear several times during a shift, but as they leave work and walk to their car, my hope was that the smile would return after they recharge in their home or other positive place.

"If that didn't happen, I wanted to know so that I could do all I could to fix what negativity they were experiencing at work. I know it sounds hokey, but I wanted laughter and a positive energy to hopefully overshadow the darker side of this profession.

"I had planned on retiring when I turned fifty-five years old in 2021. When the chief retired in 2020, I was given an opportunity and thought hard about putting in for the permanent position. I think I would have competed well. But times have changed. It's not always about the person who has been there the longest or has the most experience. I understood this and felt that after twenty-five years at BPD, eight of which were in the command staff, it was time to let new leadership come in and take the helm.

"I have occasional regrets, especially when I think of all the great times with the great people I had there. I won't rule out applying for a chief's job down the road, but after thirty-two years in law enforcement, it just felt like it was time to enjoy the other parts of my life and spending more time with my family."

I asked Mike, "Do you have any thoughts that you would like to share with those still doing the job or who might be considering it?"

He responded, "To be a cop has never been easy. When you first start your career, you and those you love are concerned about the dangers of the job and specifically the possibility of losing your life in the line of duty. But as you gain experience and utilize your training, it becomes clear that internal factors pose the same threats, if not more, to one's safety and health. Like any other profession, it is demanding and requires the right mindset to be successful.

"I would do it all over again and would still recommend someone, including family, to pursue a career in law enforcement. The job is not the same one that I began back in 1990. Like other professions, it had to change to meet the expectations from the community. For the most part, a community still appreciates and supports their police department, and I hope officers remember that."

Mike, thank you for your service!

TEN

Chief Charles Bordeleau

Ottawa Police Service (Canada): 35 Years
Retired: 35 Years of Service

Volume I and Volume II of my *Behind and Beyond the Badge* book series included people who had direct ties to my home state of Florida. One of my goals with Volume III was to include first responders from other areas of the United States and other countries.

A good friend of mine is from Canada, and I've visited family and friends there many times. It's a beautiful country, but honestly, I knew very little about policing there. My only experience with Canadian law enforcement was having the opportunity to see members of the Royal Canadian Mounted Police and their magnificent horses in downtown Ottawa.

I was talking with my friend about the progress of the book

156

and my desire to include a law enforcement officer from Canada. She told me that she had been friends with Charles for years and that they were still in contact via social media. She offered to reach out to him.

After the introduction was made, I sent Charles detailed information about the books and my purpose for writing them. I also discovered a podcast that he had been a guest on and promptly listened to it. It solidified my desire to tell his story. I asked Charles, and he agreed to participate.

The first question I always ask of people whose stories I tell is why they chose the law enforcement profession. Charles said, "I met my wife while working at McDonald's when I was in grade twelve. Her father was with the Ottawa Police Force and was in charge of detectives back then. We talked a lot about his career and the work he did. Although no one in my family had gone into policing, I found this a fascinating career and really enjoyed the stories he had to tell me.

"It was when I was in my second year at the university that I decided to try a career in policing. In 1982, my now father-in-law became the chief of the Gloucester Police Force, which was an adjacent municipality to the City of Ottawa. My father-in-law was adamant that I finish university, get my degree, and go through the rigorous hiring process to get on. He was always my role model and mentor throughout my entire career. Making a difference in the lives of people was a catalyst for me, and I wanted to do what I could to keep Ottawa safe."

Charles followed his father-in-law's advice and graduated from the University of Ottawa (Canada) in1984 with his bachelor of administration. Later, in 2010, he graduated from Royal Roads University (British Columbia, Canada) with a masters of arts in disaster and emergency management.

His policing career began in 1984 with the Gloucester Police Force, an agency with 184 members. In 1995, as a result of provincial legislation, the Regional Municipality of Ottawa-Carleton (comprised of four cities including Gloucester and Ottawa) took over policing responsibility from the cities.

Charles added, "We became the Ottawa-Carleton Regional Police Service. In 2000, all the cities in the region amalgamated, and we then became the Ottawa Police Service. When I retired in 2019, there were 1,400 sworn police officers and 600 civilians serving a population of one million in a city that spans 1,077 square miles."

Charles served in many different capacities, such as constable (both in patrol and as a detective), sergeant, staff sergeant, inspector, superintendent, deputy chief, and chief. He oversaw many different units including patrol, support services, the Ottawa International Airport, youth services, communications/9-1-1, special projects, and emergency operations.

With his experience in so many different areas, I asked Charles if he had a favorite assignment. He said, "There is no question that being a patrol officer early in my career was my favorite position. The work was amazing. I worked with a great team of officers and interacted directly with the community. Being there for members of our community in their time of need was important for me. No shift was the same. The variety of calls we dealt with kept us on our toes. One minute I could be dealing with a cow in the middle of the road in the rural part of the city and then dealing with a serious car accident followed by a serious crime. As many officers can attest, there are numerous highs and lows, and the adrenaline is always up and down.

"Having the opportunity to be the Chief of Police for Canada's nation's capital was the pinnacle of my career. It was a huge honor to serve my home community and to lead the women and men of the Ottawa Police Service for seven years as their chief.

"I had the opportunity to be president of the Ontario Association of Chiefs of Police in 2016-2017 and then vice president of the Canadian Association of Chiefs of Police in 2017-2019. I also served on the Major Cities Chiefs Association, which includes the six largest police services in Canada and about thirty of the largest police services in the United Sates.

"Policing has become more challenging over the years, and the officers on the road have it tougher compared to when I started—more accountability, more transparency, and more pressures on them that ultimately impact their mental health."

Shift work and being in a position that requires you to be on-call can be additional stressors for first responders. I asked Charles what his work schedules were like.

He responded, "While on patrol, I worked shift work including ten-hour shifts and twelve-hour shifts. I was on-call when I was in detectives and media relations.

"When I became a senior officer (inspector and above), the positions required me to carry a pager and cell phone and to be available to respond to major incidents. As chief of police, you're never really off-duty, and with the advent of technology over the years, I always had to be connected. Even when I was on 'holidays,' I was still the chief and had to be reachable."

Living in Florida, natural disasters, especially hurricanes, are always at the forefront of planning for every first responder agency. During my twenty-six-year career here, hurricanes had sadly become something we just prepared for and managed. I'm always curious about what other parts of the world have to deal with and what impact that has on law enforcement.

Charles said that working in Ottawa was no different when

it came to having to cope with natural disasters, minus the hurricanes. He explained, "In January 1998, I was the staff sergeant in charge of the Ottawa International Airport when a major ice storm struck Eastern Ontario and parts of Québec. A state of emergency was declared, and it was all hands on deck. Everyone went to work.

"During my tenure as chief of police, our community experienced two major floods (2017 and 2019) and an EF-3 tornado (2018). Our officers worked around the clock supporting fire services and the City of Ottawa Emergency Management Team that were the lead agencies."

Having spent thirty-five years in the law enforcement profession, I asked Charles what was the most difficult part of the job for him. He said, "For me, the toughest part of the job was striking the right balance between the needs of my members, the needs of my community, and my Police Services Board."

The Police Services Board is a seven-member civilian body that oversees the Ottawa Police Service. It's responsible for setting the overall objectives and priorities for the provision of police services after consulting with the chief. It is also responsible for hiring and monitoring the performance of the chief, approving the annual police budget, and preparing a business plan for the police service every three years.

Charles added, "When dealing with an event, a policy decision, or significant decision, I tried to strike the right balance between what was good for the members, the community, and my bosses (Police Service Board). That wasn't always possible and often difficult to achieve. It's like having a three-legged stool and trying to have it balanced; sometimes there's no way to do it!

"As an example, I recall an officer using force during a call, and the person suffered a serious injury. In Ontario, a third-party body, the Special Investigative Unit, is legislatively mandated to come in and conduct an investigation to determine if the officer acted appropriately or if criminal charges were to be laid. As the chief, you are prohibited by law to speak publicly to the issue until the investigation is concluded. It's not a win-win situation because the community wants answers, and the officers want to be supported publicly.

"Based on what they knew, the community wanted the officer fired, the Police Services Board was asking questions as to what training and policies we had in place that would prevent this from occurring, and my members were looking to me to support the actions of the officer involved.

"I always found these types of situations challenging because you're doing everything in your power to do the right thing, but your stakeholders are coming at the issue from three very different perspectives. Striking that right balance to maintain the trust of your members, the community, and your bosses has been a challenge. I also found times where you just had to pick a position and manage the outcome because it was the right thing to do."

Each day, every law enforcement officer strives to portray a professional demeanor when dealing with the community and co-workers. As humans first and officers second, sometimes we fail. I asked Charles what he personally did to maintain that persona.

He said, "Knowing that when a person calls the police, it's not always during the best time of their lives. What they need at that point in time is someone who is compassionate, someone who can listen, someone who shows empathy, someone who will take action and show leadership and strength under the most difficult of circumstances and maintain their professionalism. I kept reminding myself of those traits whether I was responding to a murder scene, a sexual assault, a fatal motor vehicle collision scene, the suicide of one of my officers, or standing in front of international media in response to a terrorist attack.

"I found the ability for someone to communicate effectively (talk AND listen) is the most important asset someone needs to be a great police officer. The tone a police officer uses when approaching any situation can often dictate the response and the outcome. There are many other qualities such as empathy, compassion, and the ability to apply common sense that distinguishes those who are more successful in this profession."

I've found Charles to be someone who cared deeply about the community he served and the officers and employees under his care. When I asked him what the most rewarding or fulfilling part of his thirty-five-year career was, his answer didn't surprise me.

He said, "I tried to have a positive impact on someone's life as a result of having an interaction with the police. Every time a police officer has contact with a member of the public, it's an opportunity for that officer to not only shape what that person thinks of them as a police officer but to help shape their perception of the police service and the policing profession.

"That is something I carried with me at each rank I held. Those are the interactions I found most rewarding as a street cop and hearing about them as the chief of police. When I became chief, I brought a phrase with me, which I had printed on my Chief's Challenge Coin: 'Everyone Matters.' Each member of the Ottawa Police Service matters. They have the ability to contribute in their own way to keeping our community safe regardless of the role they have in the organization. Moreover, regardless if you're a victim of crime, a complainant, or a suspect being arrested, you matter, and you deserve to be treated with the respect and dignity we all deserve."

With Charles's positive thoughts concerning police-public interactions, I asked him what the nicest compliment was that he received from someone he had helped.

He said, "I recall working as a patrol officer in 1987. I had to respond to a reported sexual assault that occurred when a high school student was walking to school one early morning. She was grabbed from behind and taken into a nearby wooded area and sexually assaulted.

"It had been raining that morning, so the woods were fairly muddy. Upon arrival at the high school, I interviewed the girl who described what had taken place, and she was able to give me some physical characteristics of the suspect. I directed a patrol colleague of mine to attend another nearby high school to ascertain if anyone matching the description might have been late for school. In fact, a young man covered with mud was late for class. He fit the description and was arrested and subsequently charged.

"I received a nice card from the victim six months later explaining how comfortable I made her feel and how supportive I was in my approach to that initial interview. That experience stuck with me throughout my career so much so that when I was appointed chief of police, ending violence against women was one of my top three operational priorities during my tenure."

I ask people to tell me about something that they would consider a career-defining moment. Some have more than one, and some can immediately relay a situation in detail and why it stands out to them. Others don't think they have one, but once they truly reflect on their career, at least one incident or person stands out.

I'm one of those individuals who has more than one incident. In hindsight, they came at different times in my career.

Charles is similar to me in that respect. He said, "I would like to outline four particularly difficult incidents that took place during my career that have one common thread—pride in the members of the Ottawa Police Service through tragedy. As a result of these four terrible events, we as a police service, including myself, and the community at large were significantly impacted by loss and tragedy.

"However, what helped get me through these incidents was how proud I was in how the men and women of the Ottawa Police Service responded to each one. The members care for each other and the community. In these days of defunding the police movement, the loss of trust and confidence in police, it's always important to ground yourself with the events that brought the community and the police together.

"The murder of Constable Czapnik is the first incident. Constable Ireneusz 'Eric' Czapnik was a proud Polish Canadian who truly enjoyed interacting with the public and serving the community. After moving to Canada in 1990, he became an active volunteer with the Polish Community Association and enjoyed playing in the Old Timer's Ottawa Carleton Soccer League. Cst. Czapnik joined the Ottawa Police Service in April 2007, following in the footsteps of his father, a police officer of thirty years in Poland. He was a husband and the father of four children—three sons and a daughter.

"Cst. Czapnik was on duty in the early morning hours of December 29, 2009, investigating an assault. After bringing the victim to the civic campus of the Ottawa Hospital, he remained outside of the emergency entrance in order to file his report. He was then approached by a man and stabbed. Despite heroic efforts from medical personnel, Cst. Czapnik, fifty-one, died of his injuries shortly after the attack. The suspect involved, who was charged and convicted of first-degree murder, was a member of the RCMP (Royal Canadian Mounted Police) who was on medical leave. He set out to kill a police officer that night.

"I was the superintendent in charge of emergency operations at the time and had the honor of leading the team that organized Eric's police funeral. It brought thousands of police officers to Ottawa from across Canada and the United States. The response from our community was truly heartwarming, and our officers, who were understandably rocked by this tragedy, held their heads high with pride in support of Eric and his family.

"A terrorist attack is the second incident. On October 22, 2014, a lone gunman approached Canadian Armed Forces Corporal Nathan Cirillo, who was on sentry duty at our National War Monument, and shot him dead. The gunman then took a vehicle across the street and entered our National Parliament Building and began indiscriminately shooting until he was gunned downed himself by an RCMP officer and the sergeant-at-arms.

"This was deemed a terrorist attack, which required a full response by the Ottawa Police Service, the RCMP, and other public safety partners. It garnered international attention and a number of operational reviews. The members of the Ottawa Police Service responded with immediacy and professionalism and as quickly as possible brought the situation under control to restore a sense of calm in our nation's capital.

"The third incident was a cold case triple homicide solved. On June 29, 2007, an unknown assailant gained entry into a high-end condominium building and brutally murdered retired Federal Tax Court Judge Alban Garon, his wife Raymonde, and their friend Marie-Claire Beniskos. The triple murder rocked our community and remained unsolved for many years until 2015, when the same assailant attempted to murder a 101-year-old war veteran, Ernest Cote, much in the same manner as he did his previous three victims.

"However, Mr. Cote survived. Through some outstanding forensic work at the scene, officers were able to match the DNA collected from a suspect at this scene to the scene of the triple homicide in 2007.

"I recall the investigative team meeting with me in my boardroom to inform me that they had solved the 2007 triple homicide. The tenacity and sheer determination of all those who worked on these cases were inspiring and brought some closure to the families and our community. I later met Mr. Cote and gave him a Chief's Challenge Coin to honor him and to let him know that he mattered. He passed away a few months later.

"The fourth incident was the OC (Ottawa-Carleton) Transpo Bus Crash. On January 11, 2019, the driver of a double-decker city bus travelling west bound on the designated transitway lost control and crashed into a bus shelter and canopy at the Westboro Transit Station. The bus was full. In total, twenty-three passengers received serious, life-altering injuries, and three people were killed.

"The police and first responders who attended to the victims that day worked under some very difficult conditions including severe cold weather, twisted metal, and a gruesome scene. Their professionalism, courage, and commitment to helping those in need was a source of tremendous pride for me as their chief."

Over the past few years, the law enforcement profession has seen a steady increase in the number of officers who die by suicide. Sadly, it is prevalent within all first responder professions as well. Mental health and the overall wellness of these dedicated professionals is finally starting to become a priority for a growing number of agencies. Many mental health professionals will tell you that the human brain wasn't wired to withstand what first responders see and deal with on a daily basis.

Having spent ten years working in our Homicide Unit, I've seen just about every possible way a human can die. It was also an up-close and personal view of what we as humans can do to each other and to ourselves. From personal experience, anyone who tells you that doing the job didn't affect them isn't being honest with you or themselves. It's simply not possible.

The first responder community still has a long road ahead, but I'm thrilled that mental health and wellness for all of them is gaining traction. I'm a huge proponent in helping make this a priority.

Since he served as a leader of a law enforcement agency, I asked Charles for his views on this topic, and I appreciated his candor. He said, "There are many parts of my career that were difficult, but I have to say that seeing the emotional impact of stress on the members, sworn and civilian, has been the most challenging part of the job.

"On September 28, 2014, one of our officers, a respected staff sergeant who was well-liked by everyone inside and outside the police service, committed suicide in his office. Making this even more difficult for us to understand was that he did this while myself and thousands of his fellow law enforcement colleagues gathered on Parliament Hill at our annual ceremony that honored officers who had lost their lives in the line of duty. This was a ceremony he attended each year with us.

"This suicide was tough on all of us. As the chief, I had the responsibility to lead the organization through this crisis and ensure all our members had the support they needed to carry on and manage through their own emotions. The impact of mental illness hits many people, and I think we are seeing the cumulative impact of stress more often these days as a profession.

"As a result of that suicide, our police service changed its approach to supporting the mental health of our members. We identified new support for them including professionals and peer support teams across the police service. We implemented a new mental health strategy and provided all our members with 'Road to Mental Readiness' training. It gave coping skills to the members and tools to supervisors so that they could recognize signs that someone might need help.

"We took aggressive steps to start changing the culture around the acceptance of mental health. Policing always thought that PSTD (post-traumatic stress disorder) was most likely associated with the impact of one major incident. We now recognize the cumulative impacts that a number of incidents can have on one's mental health. We implemented strategies to mitigate those cumulative impacts, like incident debriefings and early intervention and accessibility of support.

"A positive result is that we are openly talking about mental health, and we are trying to remove the stigma associated with this disease. We tried to make it normal to ask the question 'Are you okay?' I think it's also important to acknowledge that we have a long way to go at changing the police culture around mental health, but that journey has started."

It's important for everyone's mental health, but especially for first responders, to have an outlet to destress, decompress, and rejuvenate. I asked Charles what he did for his own physical and mental health.

He said, "Physical fitness has always been a priority of mine. I run, play golf, play hockey, cycle, and take the dog for a walk. My golfing took a back seat when I was chief, but I've made up for it since retiring! I've found physical activity to be a great stress reliever, and whatever form that takes for people is an individual decision. I've also found that having close friends outside the policing family was an important factor for me in keeping a relatively stable work-life balance.

"My wife and I also love music, and we attend as many concerts as possible. Foo Fighters is my favorite band, and we've had the pleasure of getting to know one of the band members."

Besides jumping back into golf, I asked Charles if there were any other things that he is involved with. Like so many others, Charles, even though retired, is still giving back to his community.

He told me, "Throughout my career, giving back to the community has been important. It became more significant to me as I progressed through the ranks. I served on many community boards and supported various agencies during my years of service to the community, and I maintained a number of volunteer activities which were close to my heart after my retirement. Supporting agencies that help vulnerable youth has been a strong focus of my volunteer work."

Below are some of the organizations that Charles volunteered with over the course of his career:

- No Communities Left Behind Steering Committee
- COMPAC (Community Police Action Committee) Co-chair
- Children and Youth Initiative – United Way
- Ottawa Community Development Framework Steering Committee Cochair
- Crime Prevention Ottawa Board
- United Way of Ottawa (seven years as account executive and campaign chair and in 2015 as chief of police)
- Youth Services Bureau (eight years with two years as chair of the board)

- Youth Services Bureau Charitable Foundation (six years – inaugural chair)
- Youth RecConnect (program champion)

Charles added, "Today, I remain involved as a board member for the Montfort Hospital Foundation, the Telus Community Board, the Ottawa Sports and Entertainment Group Foundations Community Cabinet, and I am the current chair of the board for Special Olympics Canada.

"Special Olympics across the world and international law enforcement share a close bond though the Law Enforcement Torch Run (LETR) that supports those athletes with intellectual disabilities and involved with the Special Olympics. I have been involved in running the Torch Run since my early days as a patrol constable, and the opportunity to join the national board representing Canadian chiefs of police came to me in 2015. I remained on the board after retirement because my passion and beliefs are strongly aligned with the values of the Special Olympics, which speak to creating inclusive communities."

As with everyone in my *Behind and Beyond the Badge* book series, I was truly honored that Charles agreed to be included and trusted me to tell his story. I asked him what he hoped people would garner from reading these books.

He said, "This is a unique opportunity for me to provide insight into my policing career. I hope to convey to the reader that regardless of your rank, the main reason we are all police officers is to keep our respective communities safe. A chief might apply a different lens to an issue impacting community safety, but the end goal remains the same. Policing in Canada has a different governance model than the United States but there are more similarities than differences in how we deliver law enforcement in our communities."

With the amazing career that Charles had and his community involvement, I asked Charles if he had received any awards. He had and told me about those that meant the most to him:

- **Deans Philos Award 2011:** The Deans Philos Award recognizes individuals who have demonstrated outstanding philanthropic achievement and social commitment.

- **Queen's Jubilee Medal 2012:** This medal was created in 2012 to mark the 60th anniversary of Her Majesty Queen Elizabeth II's accession to the throne as Queen of Canada. The Queen Elizabeth II Diamond Jubilee Medal was a tangible way for Canada to honor Her Majesty for her service to this country. At the same time, this commemorative medal served to honor significant contributions and achievements by Canadians.

- **United Way Community Builder Awards 2015:** United Way East Ontario's Community Builder Award program honors the outstanding volunteers and champions of community, those organizations, partnerships, agencies, neighborhood groups, and individuals who work tirelessly and collaboratively to make our communities better for everyone.

- **Exemplary Service Medal (2004/2014/2019):** The Police Exemplary Service Medal is a Canadian service medal for police officers. The medal honours twenty, thirty, and thirty-five years of full-time exemplary service by police officers serving with one or more recognized Canadian police forces. It is, within the Canadian system of honors, the first and highest of the exemplary service medals.

- **Officer of Order of Merit for Police Forces (2017):**
  Established in October 2000, the Order of Merit of the
  Police Forces honors the leadership and exceptional
  service or distinctive merit displayed by the men and
  women of the Canadian Police Services and recognizes their commitment to this country. The primary focus
  is on exceptional merit, contributions to policing, and
  community development. Her Majesty Queen Elizabeth
  II is the Order's Sovereign, the governor general is its
  Chancellor and a Commander, and the commissioner
  of the Royal Canadian Mounted Police is its Principal
  Commander.

I ask everyone who is in my books if they have any thoughts
that they'd like to pass on to those working in the law enforcement profession and to the general public.

Charles said, "To those serving, who have served, and who
are thinking about serving, the policing profession continues to
evolve as the composition and the expectations of society continue to change. That has always been the case. Change is in-
evitable, and it is a constant. Our profession is not immune to
it. If we stop evolving, our role in a civil society will become re-
dundant. My advice is not to stand on the sidelines and watch
change happen, but to be part of it, to help shape the future and
embrace it. Although it's often easier to be a critic of change, I
have found that it's more rewarding to be part of it. Good leaders
create an environment where people can respectfully challenge
issues, and good leaders should welcome all types of feedback
for transformation.

"Society has been critical of law enforcement as a result of
some horrific incidents that have taken place in different parts of

North America. When something terrible happens involving police in a particular community, we all feel it. I've often said 'what happens there matters here.' Policing is a worldwide family, and we share a unique bond that unites us. That is why we must continue to support each other in the face of adversity.

"However, we should not be blind to wrong doings, and we should call it out when we witness it. Having the courage of being a police officer not only means running into a dangerous situation while others run the other way; it also means having the courage to speak up when we see something wrong. That's one way we can help improve our profession. Each one of us has a role to play, whether on or off duty, in building trust and confidence in our profession and holding each other accountable.

"Policing remains a noble and rewarding profession, but it can take a toll on the human body and mind. Our uniform doesn't define us, but it is a part of who we are and what we represent. Be proud of the uniform you wear, but also be proud of who you are as a human being.

"To those outside the law enforcement profession, police officers are human beings. They are your neighbors; they're your hockey, soccer, and baseball coaches; and they care deeply about community. I recognize there are deep divides between the people in some communities and law enforcement, but we can only heal wounds and build relationships of trust if we all work together toward a common goal of mutual respect."

Family is important to Charles. He shared, "My wife has been my rock throughout my entire career. There have been some great times and some very challenging times, especially as a chief. Having grown up in a policing family certainly helped her understand, appreciate, and support my career. Her unconditional love and that of our daughter has carried me though some difficult times. My parents and my brother and sister have always been supportive and encouraged me to pursue my goals. I always sought advice and wisdom from my father-in-law who retired in 1992 after a forty-year career in policing."

Charles, thank you for your service to your community and to those who were under your care.

Charles can be reached via:
Twitter (@ChiefBordeleau)
LinkedIn (Charles Bordeleau)

ELEVEN

Sergeant Tamara Mickelson

Sacramento County Sheriff's Department (California)
Retired: 20 Years of Service

A few years ago, I began noticing posts from thinblueline4women on Twitter and began following them. The posts were always positive toward the law enforcement profession. Their website was equally positive and also provided a wide variety of resources geared toward military veterans and law enforcement officers with an emphasis on mental health wellness. It had a merchandise store, offered books for sale, and a link to a podcast.

The podcast was called *Real Life* and was hosted by Tamara Mickelson. Tamara is the creator of Thin Blue Line 4 Women.

I started listening to the podcast, and Tamara reached out asking if I'd like to be a guest. She knew about my books and wanted to talk about them. Of course I said yes. We've been friends since then. When I decided to write *Behind and Beyond the Badge Volume III*, I knew that I wanted to tell Tamara's story.

Tamara's law enforcement career began in the military. She served in the United States Air Force from 1988–1992 and was in the law enforcement side of security police. Her assignments included military bases in the United States and abroad.

Tamara was honorably discharged in 1992 but remained in the reserves until 1995. Wright-Patterson Air Force Base in Ohio was her last active-duty assignment, and she remained there until 1994, working part-time at a local drug store.

In 1994, Tamara moved back to California and became an assistant manager at another local drug store. She knew that wasn't what she wanted to do for the rest of her life and said, "My brother was a deputy for the Sacramento County Sheriff's Department (SSD), and he encouraged me to apply. I told him that I didn't want to be a cop anymore, but he assured me it was completely different than working as a law enforcement officer on a military base. I applied and was hired."

Tamara attended the sheriff's academy and graduated in October 1996. She was assigned to the Main Jail facility in downtown Sacramento where she worked for two and a half years.

In 1999, a position became available in the Crime Scene Investigation Unit. Many law enforcement agencies utilize civilian employees to staff their crime scene units while others use sworn officers. SSD staffed their CSI Unit with sworn officers and non-sworn civilian employees.

Tamara told me that she had always had an interest in that type of work so she applied for the position and was chosen. She said, "I wasn't interested in any one particular area of crime scene investigations, but I'm a very methodical and organized person and believed those traits would be a good fit for that type of work."

The CSI Unit worked twelve-hour shifts. When Tamara initially transferred to the unit, her shift was 3:00 p.m. to 3:00 a.m. Shifts were based on seniority, and eventually, she was able to transfer to the day shift, which was 6:00 a.m. to 6:00 p.m.

As a single mom, work days were a challenge. She said, "When I worked the night shift, I had to hire a nanny to stay with my daughter for the entire shift. For the day shift, I hired a morning nanny to come to my home at 4:00 o'clock in the morning so that I could leave for my shift that started at 5:00. Sacramento traffic is horrible, and it was always difficult to get to my daughter's day care by the time they closed at 6:00 p.m. She usually went to bed at 8:00 o'clock, so on workdays, it really left us with about two hours together."

In my opinion, civilian non-sworn individuals who work in crime scene units or forensic units are often overlooked when it comes to mental health and wellness training and initiatives. They are not first responders but specially trained members of law enforcement agencies who respond to horrific crime scenes and collect forensic evidence. Some departments utilize technology and scientific methods to process the evidence collected. They interpret their findings to assist the investigative teams in solving crimes and securing convictions, often testifying in court. Many agencies send the collected evidence to other laboratories for processing.

It's generic when their roles are described as processing a crime scene or collecting evidence. My intention is not to be graphic, but the fact remains that her job was extremely graphic. For instance, here is a small glimpse into what that really means. Imagine a death scene, whether it's one body or a mass casualty situation. Tamara and her colleagues would video it, photograph it, step over it and through it, measure it, touch it to collect it, and document it. It took hours, sometimes days, to properly process a crime scene.

Having spent ten years working in homicide, I couldn't have done my job without the crime scene unit. They are a critical part of the team, and I understand what they see and do. I will always be outspoken about including them in mental health and wellness initiatives.

While Tamara was a sworn officer performing these duties, she understands the toll the job takes. She said, "I spent fifteen years in our CSI Unit. After years of working crime scenes, it started to get to me emotionally. Two specific calls told me it was time to seek a different role at our agency.

"The first case was a triple homicide that involved a man who stabbed to death his sister-in-law and her two children, ages two and three. This particular scene haunts me to this day.

"The second case occurred three months later. An officer from a neighboring county was fatally shot in the head. I responded to the hospital to take photographs of him and his injuries, I collected his uniform since it was evidence, and I took inventory of his belongings. Taking inventory included emptying the contents of his pockets. He was a K-9 officer. When I removed his K-9 cards from his uniform shirt pocket, something inside of me changed. Many K-9 officers have trading-style cards, which are photos of themselves and their K-9 partner, to hand out to kids.

"I saw his smile, his courage, and his love for his K-9 partner, Yaro. I knew at that moment that I was done working in the crime scene investigation unit. I'd had enough sadness, smelled enough blood, and walked through God-knows-what too many times. I was done. Within a couple of weeks, I started studying for the sergeant promotion exam."

Tamara was promoted to sergeant and was transferred to the Main Jail where she became the administrative sergeant and the Prison Rape Elimination Act (PREA) sergeant. At that time, the jail was not in compliance with federal standards to prevent, detect, and respond to prison rape. She was tasked with bringing the department into compliance and responding to alleged rapes that occurred at the Main Jail.

Tamara said, "The work I accomplished, along with a lot of help from others, brought our jail into compliance. It was very rewarding work for me."

After eighteen months, Tamara retired from the Sacramento County Sheriff's Department with twenty years of service. The department had grown, and at the time of her retirement, the agency had 1,250 sworn officers and 660 civilian employees.

While working full time, she also managed to continue her education. In 2001, Tamara obtained her bachelor of arts degree in business management and in 2003, her master's degree in marriage, family, and child counseling. Both of her degrees are from the University of Phoenix, Sacramento campus.

Tamara told me that the most rewarding part of her job was knowing that the work she did at a crime scene was helping to bring the case to a close and bringing justice to those who deserved it.

She said, "I always took the time to answer questions when I was processing a scene, especially with domestic-violence victims. I would explain the legal process to them and why I was taking photographs of their injuries or property that might have been damaged and who would be viewing them. I was often thanked for taking the time to do that."

We have often spoken of the importance of law enforcement officers having a hobby or other interests outside of the job. Tamara said, "100 percent of my time off was with my daughter. We would run errands, go see a movie, go shopping at the mall, go out to eat, visit her grandmother, and go hiking and exploring at area parks. My daughter was my hobby. I was and still am her only parent, and so she was and is my life!"

While Tamara's daughter is her priority, I also know that she is a published author. She said, "I did pick up the hobby of writing and would dabble in it most nights after putting my daughter to bed. It was very relaxing. My first novel, *Maren's Journey,* was a product born from those nights. I self-published it in 2014, and it's available on Amazon."

Tamara classifies this book as a romance novel. I'm an avid reader but will admit, romance novels aren't usually on my to-be-read stack. But I did read *Maren's Journey* and enjoyed the story. The lead character is a flight attendant, something that I didn't realize was important to Tamara until later.

In 2020, Tamara published her second book, *Through My Eyes - CSI Memoirs That Haunt the Soul.* It was the winner in the Autobiography/Memoir category in the 2020 Best Book Awards contest sponsored by the American Book Fest and a finalist in the International Book Awards contest in the True Crime: Non-Fiction category. It's available to purchase on Amazon.

She commented, "*Through My Eyes* wasn't written to relax. It was written as a form of self-reflection and a way for me to purge horrible crime scenes from my psyche. I had learned during my master's degree coursework that writing things down versus seeing a therapist in person uses a different part of the brain and can be just as therapeutic.

"I started writing about the crime scenes I had responded to but couldn't put out of my mind. I cried many times while writing the book and, at times, would close my laptop and walk away.

But I stuck with it, and before I knew it, I had completed chapters. One day I thought about converting it into a book with the hope that citizens would learn what officers truly see and go through on a daily basis. I also thought that it could help other officers experiencing the same things I was, scenes that I just couldn't get out of my head.

"Writing this book was certainly more intense than the first one and wasn't easy to write. But putting my thoughts to paper about the worst crime scenes helped me purge it all. I just had to get it out. Now and as time goes by, I think less about the crimes, the scenes, and the victims.

"I've started another book titled *Happily Haunting Ever After* but only have two chapters written. Writing doesn't really come naturally to me, and I have to be bitten by the writing bug to sit and work on it. I'll get back to it!"

Besides writing, Tamara knew that when she retired, she still wanted to be associated with law enforcement but also thought it would be nice to have a resource for women in the profession. She said, "That's how Thin Blue Line 4 Women was born. I created a website and started selling the Thin Blue Line silicone wristbands to explore the possibility of opening an online store. I started getting requests for more law enforcement items, so I began adding products. All of a sudden, I was ordering products left and right and couldn't keep up with the demand, so I officially opened the store.

"With the website and the creation of the store, my social media following had really grown. I wanted to start interacting with them in a different capacity, so I created a podcast called *Real Life.* I'm always looking for new opportunities and love trying new things. It was important to me too as I wanted to make it about real life. I interviewed people who I thought had important stories to tell. Every guest was a first responder or a family member of a first responder. I think sharing personal stories about life helps the storyteller as much as the person listening to it."

As I mentioned at the beginning of Tamara's story, I was a guest on her podcast. It was a great, relaxed conversation over our morning coffee. I love doing podcasts, and Tamara's was no different. Eventually, Tamara stopped doing the podcast, but the episodes are still available on your favorite podcast forum.

When I asked her why she ended the show, she answered, "I stopped recording the podcast because it was taking too much time away from my daughter. I really enjoyed doing it, loved all of the interviews I did and the amazing people I met, but it is a lot of work and very time consuming."

Tamara and I stayed in touch, and she offered to sell my books on her website. But one day I got an email from her with an unexpected surprise. She told me that she had been hired by an airline and was soon to be attending flight attendant school. She added, "This is something that I've always wanted to do. When I got out of the military, I applied to become a flight attendant. However, at that time, there was a five-year hiring freeze. I was really disappointed because it was something that I'd been planning to do for a few years. That was part of the reason I applied to SSD, because my first post-military career choice was no longer an option."

Tamara started flying in January 2022. Because of her schedule, she closed her online store for a while. We kept in touch, and a few months ago, Tamara texted me and said that her flight schedule was bringing her to Tallahassee, Florida, where I live. We have talked on the phone, talked via Zoom, emailed, and texted, but we had never met in person.

I met her at her hotel. We walked to a wonderful outdoor

restaurant, had brunch, and talked until we realized people were waiting to be seated. We went back to her hotel and talked for hours until she had to leave for the airport. What an awesome day, and I'm grateful that we finally got to meet in person.

While Tamara has fulfilled a dream, the demands of her flight schedule has her away from home more than she anticipated. She ended her flight attendant career in June 2022 but said once her daughter starts college, she may go back part time. Because she is not currently flying, she has reopened her Thin Blue Line 4 Women online store.

Tamara said, "When I retired from law enforcement in 2016, my daughter was ten at the time. I moved from California to beautiful Tennessee where we've been thriving ever since. A few years later, I also helped my mom move to Tennessee, and she now lives just a few miles from us. My mother and my daughter have supported me in everything I've done, and I don't know what I'd do without them!"

I asked Tamara what she hoped people got out of *Behind and Beyond the Badge Volume III*, and she responded, "This book and your first two dive deep into the human side of first responders. People generally see the uniform and believe they're this robot-type person who was trained to respond a certain way to each call every time. But that's not reality. There's a real person behind the badge, and I hope people will have a better understanding after reading this book."

I ask those in my books if they have any thoughts they'd like to pass on and Tamara said, "As I stated in my book, *Through My Eyes,* I implore those outside the law enforcement profession to try to understand just how difficult being an officer can be. If you come across an officer in your daily routine and they aren't smiling or as cheerful as you think they should be, try to remember that you have no idea what type of call they just worked. They could have been standing over a dead body for hours. Maybe it was a five-year-old child. It could have been an animal cruelty call or a fatal vehicle accident.

"To those still working the job, THANK YOU! Please remember to take time out for yourself and do things off duty that aren't law enforcement related. Also, I think it's very beneficial to see a counselor on a regular basis even when there's nothing huge going on at work or in your life. It's like your car. Do you wait until your engine is ready to blow up to change your oil? Of course not! You change the oil on a regular basis to keep your vehicle running smoothly.

"Lastly, be good to yourself. There's only one you, and you have to live with yourself every single day. Make good choices. Keep God first in your life and pray."

Tamara, thank you for your service to your country and to your community!

If you're interested in reading Tamara's book, *Through My Eyes,* this is the link:

https://www.amazon.com/Through-My-Eyes-Memoirs-Haunt/dp/1547256389/ref=tmm_pap_swatch_0?_encoding=UTF8&qid=1655060247&sr=8-1

Tamara can be reached through her website www.thinblueline4women.com, or email her at thinblueline4women@yahoo.com.

TWELVE

Fire Marshall Tyler Van Leer and K9 Hansel

Millville Fire Department (New Jersey)
Active Duty: 10 Years of Service

I've always had an affinity for our working K-9 partners and know how hard these teams work. I'm also a dog mom and volunteer at our local shelter when I can. There are so many amazing canines across the globe working with first responders. And just like their human partners, they too put their lives on the line each and every day, serving and protecting.

While scrolling through a social media site, I came across the American Humane Hero Dog Awards. They had just held their annual awards gala in South Florida. There were winners in six categories, but one in particular stood out to me and that was Fire

Marshal Tyler Van Leer and K-9 Hansel. They had been awarded the 2021 Law Enforcement and Detection category winner.

I did a little more research on this K-9 team and knew that I wanted to include them in this book. I reached out to Tyler, told him about my books, that I was writing Volume III, and I wanted to tell his story. An email was sent giving him more detailed information, and he agreed to participate.

Tyler told me that his passion for fire service began at a young age. Every time he saw a fire truck, he got excited. For as long as he can recall, being a firefighter was what he wanted to do. After 9/11 occurred, his need to serve in some way became even stronger.

He started his career as a junior member of the Laurel Lake Volunteer Fire Department in Millville, New Jersey. This is where he was formally introduced to the fire service and first experienced the bond that forms between those who serve.

After graduating high school, Tyler married his high school sweetheart and joined the Millville Fire Department as a volunteer firefighter. He graduated from the fire academy in 2011 and was hired by the Millville Fire Department as a fulltime firefighter in 2013.

Tyler said, "When I was hired, I started as an entry level firefighter. One year later, I was promoted to fire prevention specialist. In this position, I conducted fire safety inspections in all commercial buildings and smoke alarm certification inspections in residential homes."

In 2019, Tyler attended a local event in Millville called Play Streets. It's a day of fun for the citizens with many vendors and community organizations participating. The Millville Police Department conducted a K-9 demonstration that Tyler said was the highlight of the day.

He said, "The demonstration set my mind spinning. I thought what an asset it would be to the community if the fire department had its own K-9."

Tyler approached Fire Chief Michael Lippincott about the idea. He was very supportive and told Tyler to conduct some research, learn more about the idea, and see what he would need. Officer John Butschky from the Millville Police Department was a K9 officer and a friend of Tyler's. He approached John about the idea, and as Tyler put it, "John hit the ground running."

John then put him in touch with Carol Skaziak with the Throw Away Dogs Project. Carol and her team brought a dog named Hansel to the Millville firehouse.

Tyler said, "As soon as Hansel came out of the vehicle, we locked eyes, and the bond was instant." That is an extremely short version of how Tyler and Hansel became a team.

Hansel was rescued in 2015 when he was only seven weeks old. He was part of a group of thirty-one pit bulls that were seized in Canada from a suspected illegal dog fighting operation. The dogs were initially ordered to be euthanized, but several people and organizations stepped in to intervene, and a lengthy court battle ensued.

Rob Scheinberg and his wife Danielle own Dog Tales Rescue and Sanctuary in Ontario, Canada. They were heavily involved in a public campaign (#Save the 21) to help save these dogs. Eventually, the judge ordered the dogs to be delivered to a rescue organization in Florida called Dogs Playing for Life, which was founded by Aimee Sadler. Rob ensured that the judge's orders were carried out and drove the dogs to Florida.

Ultimately, millions of dollars were spent to save these dogs.

Hansel spent approximately one year in training with Dogs Playing for Life and Canine Center Florida. Five of the rescued dogs, including Hansel and his sister Gretel, were taken to another nonprofit rescue, the Throw Away Dogs Project in Philadelphia, Pennsylvania. This organization rescues special dogs and trains them to become working, first responder K-9s.

I reached out to Carol Skaziak, the founder of the Throw Away Dogs Project. She told me that they get hundreds of emails monthly from rescues trying to find homes for their pit bulls. Her organization doesn't rescue dogs. Instead, it helps law enforcement agencies and fire departments find working dogs to add to their team.

Carol met Hansel when she travelled to Florida and met with Aimee Sadler. She returned to Pennsylvania with the five pit bulls but was worried about finding agencies that would take these dogs as working K-9s.

Officer Butschky reached out to her and told her about the Millville Fire Department wanting an arson detection dog. Throw Away Dogs had already been working with Hansel for about a year on scent detection, specifically gunpowder. They initially thought he would be a great explosives detection K-9.

Carol and her team took Hansel to Millville and met with Tyler and Fire Chief Lippincott. At the end of the visit, Chief Lippincott told her, "Let's do this."

Tyler needed time to prepare his home for Hansel, and the fire department needed time to get a vehicle ready. Approximately two months later, Tyler and Hansel became partners.

If Hansel hadn't been rescued, Carol believes that he and Gretel would have lived a horrible life as dogfighters. Carol and cofounder Officer Jason Walters donated Hansel to the Millville Fire Department at no cost.

Shortly after receiving Hansel, who was now three years old, Tyler and Hansel enrolled in the sixteen-week New Jersey

Police K-9 Association Academy. The academy was Monday through Friday, and Tyler and Hansel drove over sixty miles each day to attend.

Upon graduation from the academy, Hansel had conducted over 3,000 searches and was trained to imprint on fourteen different ignitable liquid odors. He is now a single-purpose K-9 certified only on ignitable liquids, such as gasoline, kerosene, and diesel fuel. In simple terms, people often refer to dogs like Hansel as "arson detection K-9s." Tyler and Hansel train twice a month and must recertify with the state of New Jersey twice a year.

Carol attended Tyler and Hansel's graduation from the academy. It was an emotional time. I listened to a speech that she gave that day. She is obviously passionate about what she does.

When I spoke to Carol, she said that there are plenty of pit bulls out there that would make great working K-9s. But local governments and first responder agencies are unsure about the breed and the potential liability. She and her team are dedicated to changing that perspective, and Hansel will only help with that cause.

Hansel was a welcomed member of the team. Tyler and Hansel remained on the shift A Platoon (or day shift) for one year before the fire marshal's position became available within the department, and Tyler applied. Chief Lippincott selected Tyler. He began his new position with Hansel in January of 2021 where they remain today.

Tyler told me that he and Hansel are now on-call seven days a week. Other fire and police departments around Millville have requested the assistance of Tyler and Hansel, and the duo is happy to help out.

They also interact with the community during fire prevention details. Some of the topics they teach are "Firefighters Are Our Friends," how to crawl under smoke, how to check doorknobs, and the principles and techniques of stop, drop, and roll. They also hand out smoke detectors, as well as do the monthly maintenance checks, and replacement of batteries when needed. Tyler said the kids love it, especially when he brings Hansel to their schools.

He said that very early in his career, he responded to a house fire with a man who was a paraplegic and was trapped on the first floor. He remembered crawling through the smoke-filled house with two other firefighters when he saw the man's foot. They were able to pull the man out of the house and save his life. Tyler knew then that he had made the right career choice.

Having Hansel now has confirmed that choice and enhanced his desire to serve. As a team, they can help determine if arson is involved in a fire. Then with an in-depth follow-up investigation, they can potentially remove a dangerous criminal from the community.

When speaking about the American Humane Hero Dog Award that had first brought this duo to my attention in 2021, Tyler shared, "Many dogs were nominated. When I got the email from them stating that Hansel had initially been selected for his category, I couldn't stop smiling. Then Hansel began winning each round and became a finalist. Honestly, I was shocked." Afterward, they traveled to West Palm Beach, Florida, to attend the black-tie gala and awards ceremony. Hansel even wore his tuxedo!

Besides Hansel's award, Tyler graduated from the Southern New Hampshire University with his associate of science degree in criminal justice. He is now actively pursuing his bachelor of science degree in fire administration with a concentration in fire investigation at Columbia Southern University and is anticipating a 2024 graduation.

I asked Tyler what he hoped people garnered from reading this book. He replied, "I hope people realize the daily obstacles all first responders deal with and the emotional stress that's involved. For me dealing with fires, it's tough to see people who have literally just lost everything even though we did everything that we could.

"We try to save as much property as we can and perform what we call salvage operations—trying to find and save items that are precious to these families. The emotions are heart-wrenching.

"When people come up to me and thank me for what I'm doing or tell me what I'm doing makes a difference, I feel good and that it's all been worthwhile. We are involved with so many other positive things with our community. Hansel and I also help promote breast cancer awareness and autism awareness. My niece is autistic, so for the month of April, Hansel wears a special multicolor leash that looks like puzzle pieces.

"I've known several women in emergency services who have been diagnosed with breast cancer. To show my support for them and others, Hansel wears a pink leash in the month of October.

"Both causes are important to me, and it's our way of showing support. It's also a reminder that I hope people remember that we are just like them. First responders face all of life's problems and obstacles just like everyone else. We are human too."

When Tyler is off duty, he enjoys spending time with his family and being outdoors. He added, "My wife is the most understanding and caring person I know. She understands how important my career is to me, and her continued support makes the job so much easier. My family is my backbone!"

Tyler is also a volunteer team member now with Throw Away Dogs Project. He is responsible for their Arson Detection Program and is the main contact person for fire departments interested in a K-9 program.

Tyler added, "I answer a variety of questions and am here to help any handler or fire department interested in obtaining an ignitable liquid detection K-9. We haven't placed another dog with a fire department, but we're hoping that will change. It's difficult for people and organizations to disregard all the negative attention given to the pit bull breed even when Hansel is a great example of what they can do."

Tyler and Hansel, thank you for your service!

Hansel's story can be found in greater detail on the internet. All the organizations mentioned that were involved with Hansel's rescue have active websites where you can learn more about their continuing efforts with animal rescue. Most can also be followed on social media sites.

Tyler can be reached at ThrowAwayDogsTyler@gmail.com or followed on Instagram, Facebook, and TikTok.

THIRTEEN

Telecommunicator Brendhan Sears

Lake County Sheriff's Office (Illinois)
Active Duty: 14 Years of Service

When I decided to write *Behind and Beyond the Badge – Volume I,* my initial thoughts were to tell the stories of law enforcement officers only. But as I explored the idea in greater detail, I realized that I needed to include other first responders, especially telecommunicators. Most people call them dispatchers.

Whether it was working the streets answering calls for service or working in the investigation's bureau, I couldn't have done my job for twenty-six years without them. The more I started talking with people and other dispatchers, I realized just how little those outside the first responder world, and often within it, truly know what it is they do or the toll it takes on them mentally and physically.

Some states have now officially reclassified telecommunicators as first responders, but many still don't. I do, and my books wouldn't be complete without including them.

I met Brendhan through a social media site. I noticed a post one day from *Humanizing the Headset* and a link to their website. After reading more about them, I started following their posts. A few months later, Brendhan reached out asking if I would consider being a guest on their podcast.

I've been a guest on several other podcasts, and it's something that I enjoy doing. But it's unusual when dispatchers are the main focus of the discussion. I rarely pass on a chance to talk about the books and the village of first responders, so I said yes. Talking with Brendhan and his cohosts, Norm and Kalee, was a lot of fun, and I'm grateful for the opportunity to have been on the podcast.

Brendhan and I stayed in touch, and he sent me an awesome *Humanizing the Headset* coffee mug that I now use regularly. Having talked with him and knowing a bit about *Humanizing the Headset*, Brendhan seemed like the perfect person to represent telecommunicators in this book.

In speaking with dispatchers/telecommunicators over the years, I've yet to find one who dreamed of doing this job as a child. Most seem to fall into it. Brendhan is no exception.

Brendhan's work background was in customer service and project management. In 2007, he was unexpectedly laid off from his job. Looking for a job online wasn't the norm back then but reading the employment classified ads in a local newspaper was. He found an ad for a dispatcher position with the Lake County Sheriff's Office and thought, "This sounds like the ultimate customer service job. I'm very career-oriented and think that this could be an industry that I would thrive in, so I applied."

He was hired by the Lake County Sheriff's Office in December 2007 and has been with the agency since then. The dispatch center has twenty-six full time telecommunicators that dispatch law enforcement related calls only for the unincorporated areas of Lake County. They do not handle fire or emergency medical services dispatch responsibilities.

Brendhan said, "I'm still in the same role as a telecommunicator, but now I'm also a training officer helping to train the new dispatchers. I am pursuing supervisory and management roles and would be willing to switch agencies if the right opportunity arose."

While I've known many dispatchers who have had a lengthy career reaching retirement, this profession does have a relatively high turnover rate. Physical and mental stress, burnout, shift work, and working holidays and weekends are just some of the reasons. Shifts can vary from eight to twelve hours, and some agencies have mandatory overtime to account for vacant positions.

Brendhan loves his job, and I asked him what his favorite part was. He said, "My favorite role, by far, is training. For the most part, I train our newest dispatchers exclusively on 9-1-1 call-taking, the most stressful part of training before radio training. I call this our 'sink or swim' phase. By now, they are proficient with our tools and resources like CAD (Computer Aided Dispatch) and mapping and have learned the foundation of call-taking from answering nonemergency calls before they come to me.

"Now, we take it to the next level by answering 9-1-1 calls. We gradually begin to 'simulate' very busy shifts by having them be the first one on the phones at all times and inundating them with teletypes (special computer messages) that need to go out to other agencies and entries that need to be made, such as missing persons, stolen property, and warrant hits.

"My goal is to make sure they can handle the worst of what can be thrown at us at any given time BEFORE being released from training. I need to see them work when it's absolutely crazy busy, and I need to see them do it independently.

"I love seeing a trainee's 'light bulb' moment when something finally clicks. I love the challenge of adapting my teaching to best fit their learning style. I love seeing them become independent and walking in their own path. And I love learning from them. Yes, even in teaching, you are learning!

"I also try really hard to make sure that my fellow team members are taken care of and that they feel valued. I created a resource library that includes industry-related books and magazines as well as books on leadership, industry-related nonfiction books, and even some puzzle books and adult coloring books as a de-stressor in those elusive downtimes. I created a peer-to-peer Spread Some Love board in the break room as a way to thank each other for the big and small things we do to help each other out or for a job well done.

"I make sure everyone gets a birthday card, and I stick a gift card in there for coffee. I was one of the founding members of our agency's Peer Support Team in case anyone needs to talk or vent. I've organized fundraisers for telecommunicators in need, put together fun outings, thrown pizza parties, and I revived our response to Shop with a Cop, Drink with a Dispatcher, which was a huge success and has become a *Humanizing the Headset* event.

"I support my teammates in any way and every way that I can. Last year for National Public Safety Telecommunicators Week, I canvassed our community for donations to help us celebrate and honor each other, and they did not disappoint. The response was very positive."

Knowing what our telecommunicators deal with on a daily basis, I asked Brendhan what the most difficult part of his job was. His answer wasn't quite what I expected, but I understand it.

He said, "I've been fortunate to attend several conferences and have earned some in-depth certifications, which means I have a lot of ideas. It's made me very progressive in terms of potential growth and advancement for my own center, but I'm not in a position or have the autonomy to implement change. The most I can do is put together a presentation on something I feel our agency would benefit from. Unfortunately, I haven't had as much success as I would like, and that takes its toll professionally, but I still try!"

One advantage other first responders have is that they get to see and observe the person that they are dealing with. They have the opportunity to read body language. For telecommunicators, they only have a voice to hear and interpret. That's quite a difference. I asked Brendhan what he does to remain professional while on the telephone with a caller or on the radio with a deputy.

He said, "I don't lose my cool on the phone, even in the most difficult situations. I've had to raise my voice to get a caller's attention or to get them to focus on the question at hand. There have been times where I've announced to a caller that I was disconnecting with them in nonemergency situations where their only purpose in calling was to be disrespectful.

"However, one thing I train on is how our interaction with a caller can and does have an impact on how they're going to interact with responding deputies. If I'm disrespectful, sarcastic, or rude, I've set the tone for a negative experience. Am I the catalyst for a use of force? Was someone tased because I crossed a line? If I can't keep my cool for a couple of minutes on the phone with an unruly caller, I have no business in this industry because the second I hang up the phone, that caller is no longer my problem. Their issue was never with me anyway, so there's no reason to get emotionally invested in a difficult caller.

"The same applies for the radio. I'm there to help, not be a distraction. Anything other than complete professionalism on the air can break someone's focus in an intense situation. When I've had situations where someone has been disrespectful over the air, I'll type a message to them via their in-car computer after they've cleared from their incident and just remind them that we're on the same team. If there is something we can learn from each other in the process, even better. I'm all about positive rapport with the deputies because I know it puts their mind at ease when they hear a voice over the air that they can trust. I strive to be that voice."

I really liked Brendhan's thoughts about remaining professional. I followed that with asking him what he thought was the most important quality for a telecommunicator to have.

He didn't hesitate. "Empathy. We get so caught up in the routine of certain call types that it's easy to develop a little compassion fatigue. Traffic accidents, domestic violence, threats of violence. We take so many of these calls that our response to them is second nature. Robotic.

"You know what questions to ask regardless of the situation, and it becomes easy to get lost in that routine. You've learned to take your emotion out of the equation because you know it can cloud your judgment and throw you off. And while you may have taken thousands of domestic calls in your career, this may be the first for your caller. Never forget that. They're calling for help, and you are technically helping them, but they're also seeking reassurance that everything is going to be okay even if they're not explicitly saying so."

Every first responder has that one incident or that one person that they call a career-defining moment for them. I asked Brendhan what his was.

He shared, "I took a call last year of a sexual assault of a young teenage girl that had just occurred on a bike path behind someone's residence. The caller heard the screams and went outside as it was happening. The offender took off on foot, and the caller brought the victim inside. The victim was crying hysterically.

"I've heard a lot of things in my career—suicide by gun, agonal breathing where I know someone is near death, cries of someone trapped in their house that was on fire, to name a few. I've stayed on the line while people took their last breaths, but I've never been as affected by a call than I was with this one. I got all the information I needed from the caller, but it was incredibly difficult to ask the very personal questions that needed to be asked in this situation.

"Sometimes callers don't understand the importance of these questions and become a little less cooperative and say things like *just get here!!* I don't remember that being the case in this situation, but her cries were absolutely devastating. All I could think of was my niece who was only a few years younger. When I got off the phone, I was able to get up and go outside, which isn't always the case if we're busy. Sometimes, processing calls has to wait until the phones stop ringing. I called my mom and sobbed. I've healed from that, but I'd be lying if I said I didn't get choked up retelling it to you."

I know that dispatchers often feel that they are in a thankless profession, but I asked Brendhan what was the nicest compliment he's received.

He said, "I've been on the phone with people who are threatening to take their life. These calls are the most difficult to navigate through. Some people aren't forthcoming with what's wrong. You want to gain their trust by finding some common ground to focus on, but you're going in blind when you don't know their triggers. It can be like navigating a minefield.

"But hearing that thank you from someone who you may have literally talked off a ledge is honestly the best for me. That's when I feel I've made the biggest difference and accomplished something truly meaningful."

Brendhan mentioned that he has had the opportunity to attend some specialized training classes. I asked him to go into greater detail as one in particular is how he created *Humanizing the Headset.* He is a certified training officer and was one of the first dispatchers in the state of Illinois to become CIT (Crisis Intervention Training) certified. He helped write a federal grant proposal that the agency eventually received that now requires all dispatchers and deputies to be CIT-certified.

APCO (Association of Public-Safety Communications Officials) is an international leader in training for telecommunicators. Brendhan received his RPL (Registered Public-Safety Leader) designation. This was a year-long program with several different courses structured around PSAP (Public Safety Answering Point) management and leadership. He's attended many other courses involving active shooter incidents, suicide prevention, domestic violence prevention, and dispatcher liability, to name a few.

A graduation requirement to obtain his RPL involved a community service project. This project had to benefit APCO or the telecommunicator industry at the state, regional, or national level. Brendhan created *Humanizing the Headset* (HTH) as his project.

He explained, "I wanted to create a resource and outlet for dispatchers and wanted *Humanizing the Headset* to be something unique but also sustainable. It has evolved through trial and error into something I'm very proud of. We have a website with links to our podcast, blog, memorial for fallen dispatchers, our shop with some great items for sale, and a tab for resources.

"Wellness and self-care are huge issues for us and our profession, and we spend a good amount of time focusing on that area. We also celebrate and honor the wonderful things that dispatchers are doing not only for the profession but also for their communities. I feel it's the perfect representation of our namesake. The positive response to HTH has been amazing, and it grew so much that I had to bring on two of my coworkers to help. We've grown to a team of six. HTH is a large undertaking and is really a full-time job. Absolutely nothing happens without this great team!

"We also try to be involved in the community, although COVID made that difficult during the past few years. Fortunately, we started volunteering again this year with Feed My Starving Children. They are a nonprofit that involves hand-packing meals that get shipped to children in need all over the world. We plan it in advance so that we can open it up to other dispatchers who are interested in giving back as well. It's really a great cause, and we have a lot of fun doing it."

As busy as Brendhan is, I asked him what he does to de-stress or rejuvenate. He said, "I used to be an avid musician and vocalist, but my schedule doesn't allow for that much anymore. I am frequently called to perform the National Anthem and won a contest to perform it at our telecommunicator state conference last year. I still have a lot of musical 'energy,' if you want to call it that, so in place of performing, I started composing orchestral and band music mostly. I do get asked on occasion to transcribe something by ear, which is a challenge I really have a lot of fun with.

"Transcribing is writing out the notes for music that doesn't have any sheet music available. I've done it for Chicago-area producers looking to have their tracks performed by live musicians. The software I use also plays the music back with real instrument sounds, so I've used it to score short and large orchestral works. It can be used just for the sound as well. It can very time consuming as I have to listen to a track very closely to figure out the instrumentation, and then I have to write each part out note by note. I feel it helps keeps my mind sharp.

"I compose original music and do arrangements of others as well. Believe it or not, I actually wrote the intro music for our podcast, and if you think it sounds a little tongue-in-cheek, you're right! I meant it to sound like something of a throwback to what you'd hear when you turned on the news years ago. I've even done a Halloween and Christmas variation just to have a little more fun with it. Sometimes, I think it's good not to take ourselves too seriously!

"I spend as much free time as I can composing. A goal that I've made for myself this year is to finally get published.

"It's important for us to find ways to destress. Our jobs are stressful, and it isn't always just the calls that make it that way. Other issues, such as faulty equipment or resources that aren't always available, add to that stress.

"Not to mention the stressors outside of work and with COVID always looming in the background. I actually just wrote a blog on my self-care journey for the HTH website. As the sayings go, you can't pour from an empty glass, and if you don't make time for your wellness, you'll be forced to make time for your illness. And while that may sound cliché or even a little tacky, when your glass is empty, these sayings really resonate with you. You absolutely have to make time for yourself."

I asked Brendhan what he hoped people would gain by reading the *Behind and Beyond the Badge* book series. He said, "I can't tell you enough how I appreciate you getting a dispatcher's perspective. Many people don't understand what it is we actually do, let alone the experiences that we have. And that includes the people we support. PTSD (post-traumatic stress disorder) is very real in our industry, and we don't need to be IN a situation in order to be traumatized by it.

"Our minds always go to the worst-case scenario, so what we visualize in our heads while experiencing these calls in real time is often much worse that what actually is happening. As the door opens for Next Generation 9-1-1, a new and evolving software, it adds video capabilities. Some agencies already have the ability to literally watch things as they unfold. There has never been more of a time in the history of 9-1-1 than there is right now to classify us as first responders."

Brendhan comes from a family that includes other first responders—firefighters, dispatchers, nurses, and an uncle who is currently the Assistant Director of Fire and Life Safety at a large university in Chicago. They all understand what it's like to miss holidays or other family functions due to work schedules.

I asked Brendhan if he had any thoughts that he'd like to share with others in his profession or those outside the first responder world. He said, "For the non-dispatcher readers, and that includes other first responders, there's a lot we do that you don't know about. For our callers, there are specific reasons that we ask the questions that we do, and there's a whole other side to our job that has absolutely nothing to do with answering the phones or talking on the radio.

"Some people have these perceptions of what it means to be a dispatcher. I'm not sure if it's from something fictional they've seen on TV or if it's just their personal idea of what they think we do, but not every agency does things the same way. We shouldn't let those preconceived notions of how you think we should be doing our job get in the way of how we actually do it.

"We need verbal confirmation on questions like 'Are they conscious?' or 'Are they breathing?' We can't make assumptions on an event that we are not a witness to. Misinterpretations have consequences, and those consequences include permanent disability or death. So please remember that the time to ask why we do what we do should not be DURING the emergency you are calling to report. That merely delays getting the answers we need for the help we are working hard to provide, even if it may not seem that way in the moment. Help has been on the way, and our questions aren't slowing them down.

"People outside of our industry, and even some within, have called us lazy because of some misconception that we're always sitting back with our feet up on the consoles. While the vast majority of our job is 'in the moment,' the reality is that it's very seldom that those phones aren't ringing. Most dispatch centers answer both nonemergency and emergency calls. We get calls that don't require police, fire, or rescue response and dozens of calls for the same accident until help is on scene, and we get calls that need to be transferred to other agencies.

"Who do you think people call when they don't know who else to call? US! 'What time is trick or treating?' 'What time is sunset?' 'When will my electricity be restored?' 'What is the forecast for today?' 'Are the bars open late because of the holiday?' Yes, those are actual questions that we get from people who call in. We may not be dispatching deputies to any calls at the moment, but that doesn't mean we're not still rocking and rolling in the communications center!

"We're also making calls, pinging phones of missing people, getting tow trucks started to a scene, starting fire or rescue, or advising appropriate agencies about flooding, animal pickup, road hazards, coroners, just to name a few. If you've ever wondered how the right people appear on the scene of even the strangest incidents, that was the result of all us hard at work!

"There's also the administrative side. Every first responder has paperwork. If there is a record for something, odds are we had a hand in creating or maintaining it—missing persons, any type of missing or stolen property, orders of protection, warrants, and messages from agencies who have had contact with or found any of the aforementioned. Many agencies have a dedicated person to handle all of this, and larger agencies (like Chicago, for example) have a separate division within that exclusively handles this side of the job.

"In the event of a large-scale event, 9-1-1 is not the number to call solely to satisfy your curiosity. Our county had a large plant explosion just outside our police jurisdiction. We felt it several miles away in our dispatch center. The response overwhelmed the 9-1-1 system as we only have a finite number of lines at our disposal. The calls began rolling over into several other dispatch centers, including ours. Hundreds of them.

"Not one single person I spoke to was involved or in any immediate danger. Most of them were also miles away from the explosion. They just wanted to know what was happening. This potentially comes at the expense of those who are involved not being able to reach us. We need to keep those lines open for them. In an unexpected large-scale event, there is no way we're going to have immediate information to share because we are relying on those involved to call and tell us what is happening.

"The chances of that are severely impacted by those calling on 9-1-1 just to ask what happened or the media bombarding us on the nonemergency lines for the same. As soon as we know something, your agency's Public Information Officer will alert the media and share information on their social media pages, which I hope in this day and age, every agency has.

"Thank you to all the amazing dispatchers out there holding it down at their agencies, many of whom are facing critical staffing shortages that make sixteen hour shifts the norm, keeping you away from your family and friends even longer. You're the real MVPs. Please remember to practice self-care anyway you can. It doesn't have to be some grand gesture like a weeklong Caribbean cruise.

"It can just be you sitting silently in your car for ten minutes after your shift to mentally wash the day off you so that you're not bringing potential negative energy back to a family who missed you and who you missed. Read a little bit. Meditate for a while. Write in your journal. Listen to some music. Do the things you need to do to recharge and refill your cup, even if it's just for twenty minutes a day."

Thank you, Brendhan, for your service to your community!

Brendhan can be reached at brendhan@humanize911.com.

HTH is also on Facebook (public page and a private page for first responders and industry leaders), Instagram, Twitter, and LinkedIn.

FOURTEEN

Victim Advocate Fawn Bascom

Tallahassee Police Department (Florida)
Active Duty: 14 Years of Service

I met Fawn many years ago while still working at the Tallahassee Police Department (TPD). She was a full-time dispatcher with our agency, but that isn't where her professional journey began.

Fawn graduated from Florida State University (FSU) with a bachelor of science degree in social work. She started her career in banking, and oddly, that's how she became an integral part of the law enforcement family.

She said, "I met a ton of law enforcement officers while working at one of our local credit unions. Many of them encouraged me to become an officer. Eventually, I applied and was hired as a police officer with TPD in 1999. I graduated from the academy and was two weeks into the third phase of the field training officer program when I realized policing wasn't for me.

"A supervisor asked me if I would be interested in becoming a dispatcher. I had bills to pay, so I said yes and stayed at TPD as a full-time dispatcher until 2006."

She left TPD and accepted a dispatcher position at the Florida Highway Patrol for one year and then moved to the Florida Department of Corrections as a classification officer. Fawn told me that she knew she wanted to do more with her career, and dispatch wasn't it. At that point, though, she didn't really know what she wanted to do.

A couple of prior interactions with TPD's Victim Advocate Unit led her to exploring that avenue as a possible career path. She explained, "It goes back to my time in the academy. Jill McArthur, a victim advocate at TPD and my mentor, did a presentation on domestic violence. During that time, one of my classmates was in an abusive relationship with a law enforcement officer. We were trying to help her, but she was resistant. During the presentation, Jill was saying some of the same things we were telling her about this guy.

"At the end of the class, we talked to her again, and she made the decision to report the abuse. I reached out to Jill for help, and she did an amazing job walking my friend through the process. I never forgot this.

"Fast forward to my time being a dispatcher. While I was in dispatch, one of my trainers was killed in a traffic crash. Those on her shift were called in for a debriefing. We met with a victim advocate who sat with us and helped us process the loss.

"I decided to volunteer with Jill. On my days off, I would go to the Victim Advocate Office at TPD and follow up with victims on the phone. I didn't have face-to-face contact, but it was enough for me to decide that this was what I wanted to do."

I supervised TPD's Homicide Unit for ten years. During that time, I also supervised the Victim Advocate Unit for several years. The unit was staffed with four full-time advocates. The turnover rate was low, but when we did have a vacancy, it was a highly competitive hiring process.

Fawn applied for the Victim Advocate Unit three times, and on her third attempt, she was hired. She has been a member of the unit since 2008, two years after I retired. TPD and the Tallahassee community are fortunate to have a Victim Advocate Unit that is staffed with four full-time advocates. There are law enforcement departments who have part-time employees, some who utilize volunteers, and still others who have no advocates at all. For me, our advocates were an integral part of the team.

The advocates at TPD are first responder advocates. They respond to active scenes of violent crimes, provide crisis support, grief support, make death notifications, transport victims to safe shelter, help obtain financial assistance when needed, provide information on community resources, and act as a liaison between law enforcement and survivors. They also assist and support victims during court proceedings and with obtaining domestic violence injunctions. Their interaction with victims or families can often last several years, depending on the pace of the criminal justice system.

Our Victim Advocate Unit was and still is housed in the Criminal Investigation Bureau. They work closely with all of the investigative units, the Traffic Homicide Unit, and the Patrol Division. The advocates are on-call just like the detectives, available to handle all situations requiring their assistance after normal business hours. And honestly, they do so much more.

I wasn't sure if the hiring requirements and training had changed since I retired, so I asked Fawn.

She answered, "I'm not sure what other agencies require, but TPD requires an applicant to have a four-year college degree in social work, psychology, criminal justice, or some related discipline.

"Most victim advocates in Florida also complete a Victim Services Practitioner Designation course that is offered by the Florida Attorney General's Office. It's a forty- hour class that covers the basics of victim services such as crisis intervention, death notifications, and domestic violence. Every four years, we complete a refresher course. If funding allows, we attend yearly conferences hosted by the National Organization of Victim Assistance (NOVA).

"Our unit also attended a forty-hour training class to be a part of the Florida Crisis Response Team (FCRT). The FCRT is a group of statewide practitioners who respond to natural disasters such as hurricanes and to other mass casualty incidents such as the Pulse Nightclub shooting and the Marjorie Stoneman Douglas incident. As you can see, we are involved with so many things."

With all that they do, I asked Fawn what the most difficult part of the job was for her. She responded, "The most difficult part is not what most people think. Yes, it's hard watching the worlds of innocent people crumble, but I've gotten used to that.

"The hardest part of the job is explaining the reality of what an investigation entails versus what people see on television. First responders are the first contact that people have with the criminal justice system. Cases are not always wrapped up in the first forty-eight hours. These cases can go on for days, weeks, months, and even years! DNA is not always present at a crime scene. Witnesses don't always want to talk. There may not even be a witness. And even when all of these things do line up, it still takes the detectives time to put everything together to make an airtight case.

"The last few years have not been kind to law enforcement. Even though I don't wear a uniform, I still represent an entity that some people don't like or trust. The constant scrutiny can be exhausting, frustrating, and scary. It can be difficult having conversations about why a case hasn't been solved. We don't care what race you are, how much money you make, or who you know. We care about finding the bad guy and maybe, just maybe, finding the answers so many families seek: Why did this happen? But that doesn't always occur. Being a person that wants to always 'fix it,' it's very hard to have to leave something broken or unresolved."

Law enforcement agencies train and prepare for mass casualty incidents. It is no longer a situation of *if* such an incident occurs but sadly, *when*. Many communities have experienced more than one. Tallahassee is one of those communities.

As I interviewed Fawn, I recalled one such incident that occurred in November 2014 on the FSU campus at the Strozier Library. A more recent incident occurred four years later in 2018.

A mass shooting had occurred at the Hot Yoga studio during a yoga class. Six women were shot, two fatally. A male was pistol-whipped before the shooter took his own life.

While everyone sees the law enforcement and emergency medical team responses on the news, there is so much more that happens behind the scenes. TPD was the lead agency tasked with investigating the incident.

As a member of TPD's Victim Advocate Unit, Fawn explained their role that night. "I did not respond to the scene, but another advocate did. Another remained at the police station, and I responded to the hospital. It was utter chaos at the emergency room.

"Because there were several injured people, there were friends and families of everyone involved there. I didn't know the status of most of the injured, so initially, I worked on notifying the family of one of the deceased (an FSU student) and her sorority sisters who were at the emergency room.

"I worked with the victim advocate from FSU and asked her to work with the girls while I spoke with the family of the deceased. I think we worked until about four that morning and then were back in the office at eight.

"The next day, the FSU advocate and I spoke with the family of the deceased student when they arrived from out of town. We provided case information and answered their questions letting them know how the investigation would proceed from this point forward.

"One of my advocate coworkers and I went to the hospital and met with other injured survivors from the class. We provided our usual services of crisis/trauma/grief support, but honestly, most of the victims were still in shock and still trying to process what had happened on top of dealing with their injuries. So we kept those initial visits brief.

"The mental health service providers in our community stepped up that weekend. We were able to compile an extensive list of local therapists that specialized in trauma. The majority of them were offering their services for free to the survivors and the families of the deceased. I am very thankful to them for doing that. We made the initial connections between the local survivors with those therapists and coordinated with law enforcement advocates in other communities to get services for those who lived outside of Tallahassee.

"We worked with the Florida Attorney General's Office on all of the Victim Compensation applications that were being submitted. A dedicated analyst in their office processed the applications immediately, so there was no lapse or delay in services. To put this into perspective, all of this happened within the first forty-eight hours of the incident occurrence.

"Community vigils were held, and we made sure that there were victim advocates available during those times in case anyone was in need of assistance. We also coordinated with the victim advocate from the FBI and another local advocate to provide a crisis debriefing for the staff of the yoga studio.

"This incident was a little different for me because I often took classes at that yoga studio. I thought about where I normally placed my yoga mat when I attended a class. It hit me hard—I could have been one of those victims. Once the incident broke on the local news, my phone began blowing up with calls and text messages. Friends knew that I took classes there and were worried. The only thing at the time I could reply was that I was fine and that I was working.

"Even though you prepare for this from a work stance, it's still hard to comprehend when it does happen. And at a yoga studio? I can reflect on how this affected me, but nothing I experienced can compare to the families of the deceased, the survivors, and the studio staff. Those individuals are amazing, and I consider it an honor to have met and worked with them."

While first responder professions can and do have difficult challenges, there is always something that keeps these people coming back the next day. For Fawn, she shared one of those positives.

"When I'm working with a family in reference to a criminal situation, I explain how an investigation works and the steps that need to be taken, and I ask them to trust the process. Trust that the officers are going to do the right things and give their best effort. When that process works and a suspect is arrested, when someone is now being held accountable, it's the best feeling.

"One of the nicest compliments I've received was after working a suicide incident. The entire time I was making the death notification to the mother, she just sat there and glared at me. She barely spoke to me, and when she did, her responses were short. I spent about two hours with her.

"When I was getting ready to leave, she told me that her son was an addict and that he had had many encounters with law enforcement, none that were pleasant. She then said to me that she had a very negative view of law enforcement until she met me. When I left, she thanked me for being there with her."

Fawn has been the recipient of several awards including the Florida Attorney General's Victim Advocate of the Year in 2010. Also, in 2018, TPD's Victim Advocate Unit received the Florida Attorney General's Distinguished Victim Services Unit Award for the yoga studio incident, and the Charles Morris Victim Advocate Unit Award presented by the Big Bend Victim Advocate Coalition.

Fawn is very clear on her work-life balance and believes it is essential in staying grounded. She explained, "When I'm not at work, I don't want to see it or think about it. My work cell phone is turned off and stays in the car. I also have several friends who are not related to my job, something I feel is important."

I asked Fawn if she had any thoughts that she'd like to share with those outside the first responder world.

She said, "I really want people to know that I am human too and so are all first responders. Even though we encounter terrible and unimaginable things, we go on. We give each case our full attention and effort, and then we go home. Sometimes I feel that it's unfair that I get to go home to my loved ones when I just left the scene where someone just lost their loved one or loved ones. It's not what I signed up for, yet it is. I always tell people that I love my job, but I hate what I have to do."

Fawn and her husband Rob have been together for nine years and married a little over a year ago. She described Rob as her rock, the person who keeps her grounded and is her voice of reason.

Thank you, Fawn, for your service to your community.

FIFTEEN

Sergeant Julien Ponsioen

Metro Vancouver Transit Police: 8 Years
British Columbia Ambulance Service: 21 Years
Active Duty: 29 Years of Service

I was scrolling through Twitter and noticed a retweet by someone that included a short video called *Coffee with a Cop.* I clicked on the video and watched. It was informative and I thought a great way to educate the public. The videos were narrated by Constable Julien Ponsioen with the Metro Vancouver Transit Police. I watched several of his videos and began following him on Twitter and Instagram.

Several months later, I reached out to Julien, introduced myself, and asked if he'd be interested in letting me tell his story in *Behind and Beyond the Badge – Volume III.* I'm honored that he said yes.

Julien told me that he had always wanted to be a police officer, but growing up in small communities, his primary exposure was to the Royal Canadian Mounted Police (RCMP). Many of these officers are assigned to small towns and work by themselves.

At that point in his life, he was young and felt isolated in his struggle to accept himself as a gay man. Living and working in a remote area by himself wasn't appealing to him.

He wanted to help people and thought that emergency medical services was a career that would suit him. He was hired by the British Columbia Ambulance Service and obtained his Primary Care Paramedic certificate through the Justice Institute of British Columbia. For the first seven years, Julien worked in several small communities within British Columbia. Once he moved to the Metro Vancouver area, he was exposed to many different municipal police agencies.

Julien said, "Once I saw that there were so many law enforcement options, I started to explore the idea of going back to my first love and becoming a police officer. I had become a paramedic supervisor, a position that I enjoyed, so I never acted on it. That changed when I had was notified that my role was changing, and for me, it wasn't for the better.

"One day, my boss came into my office. He put his feet up on my desk, sat back in the chair, and said, 'I'm changing your job description.' He told me that I was no longer going to be working on the street as a supervisor, but instead, I was going to manage the dispatch center.

I responded by seeking clarification. "I want to make sure I understand this correctly. You want me to come off the street as a supervisor, where we have several hundred paramedics working with only two other supervisors, and move into the dispatch center where we have thirty people working and five supervisors?"

He asked if I had an issue with that. I just reminded him that he was the boss and that I would do whatever he needed to be done. But that night, I went home and decided that it was time to change careers; I was no longer happy, and this was the final push I needed.

"A short time later, I submitted my application to the Metro Vancouver Transit Police. The real decision for me was when they offered me a recruit constable position. I would be walking away from a job that I worked at for twenty-one years and would be making less money initially. But this was this right decision for me.

"I took the position and handed in my resignation to the British Columbia Ambulance Service. I then obtained my Police Constable Certificate from the Justice Institute of British Columbia, and I've never looked back! This has been a great journey for me, and I believe I've helped create a positive and open atmosphere between my job and the community."

Julien started his new career as a patrol constable. He later became a neighborhood police officer. While in the latter role, he created a Community Policing Centre that was focused on the transit system. This was done during the COVID pandemic. The challenging part of starting the volunteer program during this time was that he needed to interview, hire, and engage volunteers without physically being with them. He successfully opened the doors to the public in February 2020 with strict COVID protocols.

He was promoted to sergeant in 2021 and is now the operational planning sergeant. When I asked Julien what his favorite position in his career thus far has been, he said, "I enjoy what I do now. It's very challenging to meet with different cities and agencies and plan resources for different events. However, I would say my time as the neighborhood police officer was my favorite as I had opportunities to start up a community office, train, mentor volunteers, and be a part of many different events around the area."

Julien is the first law enforcement officer I've had in the *Behind and Beyond the Badge* book series who works for a transit police agency. According to their website, the Metro Vancouver Transit Police (MVTP) is the only dedicated police service in Canada that is focused on reducing crime and disorderly behavior relative to the public transportation system. They have 184 officers and eighty-four civilians who are responsible for 148 kilometers of railway, sixty-three stations, 2,000 buses with 245 bus routes, and one ferry route that is spread out over 1,800 kilometers (roughly 1,118 miles). They serve twenty-one communities.

Transit police officers are designated provincial police officers, which means they have full police powers throughout the province of British Columbia, the same as municipal officers in British Columbia. As fully qualified officers, their authority is not restricted to transit property or transit-related incidents only.

Their beat-style policing allows them to build partnerships and relationships with passengers, transit staff, government partners, and other police partners. They are committed to providing a safe and secure environment for those who use and work with public transit.

Julien said, "Every municipal police officer in British Columbia is designated as a provincial police officer so our authority extends to the provincial borders. Part of my current role is to help develop emergency plans for different types of events. In the event of a disaster or large-scale incident, all members of the MVTP would be called upon to assist, and this could be within any of the twenty-one different municipalities we are in."

In following Julien on social media, it became apparent to me that he enjoyed engaging with the public, so I asked him if this was why he started *Coffee with a Cop.*

He said, "I started this in 2017 as a way to engage with commuters. My chief and I did a physical, in-person version at our Waterfront Station, but not many of them wanted to stop and chat. We had coffee, but they took the free coffee and continued on to work. I realized that if I wanted to connect, I had to do it on their terms. I had to go digital and be on their phones while they were riding the transit system. It started with simple safety tips and information in one minute or less and has grown to longer videos.

"People actually liked it and started to follow me. I now have people following me and *Coffee with a Cop* from all over the world. I've opened it up and engage through their questions and with different topics. Most people like it, but I do get negative comments from time to time. Overall though, it's very positive."

Julien is passionate about his community and has volunteered for twelve years with an organization called Cops for Cancer. He said, "This group is made up of peace officers and other emergency services personnel who cycle in different areas around British Columbia and Ontario to raise money for childhood cancer research and support services at the Canadian Cancer Society. I have personally raised over $21,000.00, but I have been part of a team that has raised over $5.5 million."

On Julien's social media, he is often seen in his uniform with a police patch that is in the rainbow colors, a symbol of the LGBTQ community. The MVTP is an inclusive agency, and this patch is approved to be worn. As a member of the LGBTQ community, Julien knows that there is often mistrust between that community and law enforcement. He said, "It's important to me to be able to connect with members of the LGBTQ community to show them that I'm there for them and that they can feel safe with me. But I also want to show young queer people that they too can be police officers.

"The patch has generated a lot of comments, both positive and negative, with the vast majority being positive. Hate is certainly out there so I made a TikTok video in the spring of 2022 that addressed this. The video took off and has been viewed over 300,000 times. I was on one of our national news channels and several radio stations. When I'm out on the street, I don't receive one negative comment; in fact, it has created a lot of positive conversations and comments of support.

"I'm also active with a nonprofit group called Out on Patrol. It's for law enforcement officers and allies who work with police agencies. We do educational presentations and award scholarships to students who want to start a career in law enforcement, and we work to connect with the local LGBTQ communities."

When I asked Julien what his favorite part of the job was, his answer came as no surprise. "Connecting with young people is by far the most rewarding part of my job. Unfortunately, there are a number of anti-police groups, negative social media posts, and an overall negative sentiment out there. For me, being able to connect with young people helps develop a positive relationship to show that police are friendly, approachable, kind, and compassionate. I want to help build a level of trust in our police services. I believe that it's important for officers to be compassionate. We deal with so many different aspects of society, and we need to be able to do that in a caring, nonjudgmental way."

I asked Julien why he agreed to let me tell his story. He said, "I want to help inspire others to get into law enforcement, to help make a real difference. As an openly gay male, I want to see them come into the field and promote change in law enforcement and the LGBTQ community. There are very few openly gay men in the policing world, and I want to see that change. I want to be someone who helps others follow a career path that they want and to show that they do not need to fear whether they will be accepted or not."

Having spent twenty-one years as a paramedic and eight and half years as a law enforcement officer, Julien has, at times, seen the unthinkable. In one of his social media videos, he talks about being asked to describe the worst thing he has seen. I believe that every first responder has been asked that question at least once. Julien's answer was simply that he wasn't going to answer that question. He went on to explain that when you ask that question, you are actually asking that first responder to relive that particular incident.

I know that I've thought that same response but never verbalized it. I appreciate him doing just that! Julien further explains that he has sought mental health therapy to help him deal with some of those very scenarios that people often want him to discuss. I'm proud of him for sharing that as well.

It's important for law enforcement officers and all first responders to have time to destress and rejuvenate, and Julien shared what he likes to do away from work. "I used to have a sailboat that I would take out for a few hours or a few days. I've since sold that and focus more on house renovations. I really love to see something from start to finish; it gives me a great sense that I've accomplished something important. I also like to hike, bike, paddleboard, travel, and basically anything that gets me outside. All these activities help me focus my mind on other things outside of work and keep my brain and body active."

In 2021, Julien was awarded the Deputy Chief's Commendation for creating the Waterfront Community Policing Centre, the first ever volunteer community policing center for a transit system. In October of 2022, he was a guest speaker at the International Conference on Crime Observation, Criminal Analysis, and Best Practices held in Paris, France. He spoke on two topics: the Waterfront Community Policing Centre and the impact it's had on the transit system and the Out on Patrol organization and its positive impact between law enforcement and the LGBTQ community.

Julien, thank you for your service as a paramedic and as a police officer.

Julien can be reached via Instagram, Twitter, TikTok, and LinkedIn at:
https://www.instagram.com/sgtjponsioen/
https://twitter.com/SgtJPonsioen
https://www.tiktok.com/@sgtjponsioen
https://ca.linkedin.com/in/julien-ponsioen

ABOUT THE AUTHOR

Donna Brown

Donna Brown was raised on the East Coast of Florida and moved to Tallahassee to attend Florida State University. After graduating with her degree in criminology, she was hired by the Tallahassee Police Department where she spent the next twenty-six years serving her community. Ten of those years were as the sergeant supervising the department's Homicide Unit.

In 2017, Donna's first book, *Behind and Beyond the Badge – Volume I,* was published, and in 2018, *Volume II* followed. Her books are a collection of individual stories about law enforcement officers and other first responders, such as firefighters, EMS personnel, dispatchers, crime scene/forensic technicians, and victim advocates. They make up what she calls her "Village of First Responders." Both books have won numerous awards for excellence in nonfiction and true crime literary genres.

Donna believes that most people see only a badge, but they need to get to know the person behind and beyond the badge. Humanizing the badge has become Donna's passion and has led to many public speaking engagements and guest appearances on numerous podcasts.

The *Behind and Beyond the Badge* series is about the message "My books don't have the power to change minds, but perhaps by offering a different perspective, I can open them."

Donna is married and together with her spouse, they enjoy playing golf and spending time with friends, family, and their fur babies.

Lightning Source UK Ltd.
Milton Keynes UK
UKHW011851090223
416719UK00004B/393/J